Advance Praise for *The Actor's Mindset*

"This book is about so much more than acting. It's filled with straight, insightful knowledge about how to live as an artist of integrity and substance. Craig doesn't pull any punches and thank goodness. I wish I had gotten this kind of brutally honest and comprehensive advice when I was starting out. He saves you (hopefully) from learning the hard way! He covers IT ALL!"

—**Kathryn Erbe**, Tony Award nominee and
star of *Law and Order: Criminal Intent*

"I loved it! More than a book about acting, it's a guidebook to living fully. A guidebook to believing you are enough, just as you are. It will sit on my nightstand always, so it can bring me inspiration whenever I forget why I decided to become a storyteller in the first place, and how lucky I am do to what I do every day."

—**Beth Behrs**, People's Choice Award nominee and
star of *The Neighborhood* and *Two Broke Girls*

"Craig's book is full of the important lessons he's been teaching me from the beginning of my career. While most acting books focus on either the art *or* the business of the entertainment industry, this book looks at both, helping all actors be prepared for both before *and* after the red carpet. It will be the secret weapon for many actors for years to come."

—**Dallas Liu**, best known for roles in *Avatar: The Last Airbender*,
Shang Chi and the Legend of the Ten Rings, and *PEN15*

"Craig Archibald has brought us a powerful, charming, and accessible book about storytelling, the human condition, and where the art of acting and business meet. His love, respect, humor, and mastery emanate like heat coming from each page, leaving the reader wondering why it took so long to see this type of clarity in one of the world's oldest professions. I consider this a must-read for actors, entrepreneurs, and all souls bold enough to live a hero's journey."

—**Les McGehee**, author of *Plays Well with Others: A 'Grown-Up' Handbook of Improvisation and Play* and co-creator of *The ONE Thing* Trainer Certification program (based on the bestselling book *The ONE Thing* by Gary Keller and Jay Papasan)

"What I most admire about Craig is that he's been in the trenches. He is an actor, he's worked in NY theater, and on film, at the highest levels. He is one of us. He's a peer. He's not dogmatic. He's not a guru. He's a guide. He knows the mountain. And if you're disoriented or feeling like you don't have the gas to make it up—he'll hold out his hand and tell you very softly, 'You can do it. Let me help.' Craig brings you back to the basics—and make no mistake, no matter which 'school' of acting you studied, or what your process is, there are basics. His philosophy of taking anything and everything, including (especially) challenges, and finding a way to use them and turn them into positives, is career altering! The Mindset is everything!"

—**Michael Gladis**, two-time SAG Award winner and star of *Mad Men* and *Penny Dreadful: City of Angels*

THE ACTOR'S MINDSET

THE ACTOR'S MINDSET

Acting as a Craft, Discipline, and Business

Craig Archibald

APPLAUSE
THEATRE & CINEMA BOOKS

Guilford, Connecticut

APPLAUSE
THEATRE & CINEMA BOOKS

An imprint of Globe Pequot, the trade division of
The Rowman & Littlefield Publishing Group, Inc.
4501 Forbes Blvd., Ste. 200
Lanham, MD 20706
www.rowman.com

Distributed by NATIONAL BOOK NETWORK

British Library Cataloguing in Publication Information available

Library of Congress Cataloging-in-Publication Data

Names: Archibald, Craig, author.
Title: The actor's mindset : acting as a craft, discipline and business / Craig Archibald.
Description: Guilford, Connecticut : Applause, [2022] | Includes index.
Identifiers: LCCN 2021039135 (print) | LCCN 2021039136 (ebook) | ISBN
   9781493063345 (paperback) | ISBN 9781493063352 (epub)
Subjects: LCSH: Acting. | Acting—Vocational guidance.
Classification: LCC PN2061 .A73 2022 (print) | LCC PN2061 (ebook) | DDC
   792.02/8—dc23
LC record available at https://lccn.loc.gov/2021039135
LC ebook record available at https://lccn.loc.gov/2021039136

For my parents, Florence and Cameron Archibald, whose love, integrity, fairness, humor, and sense of community have made me who I am.

In loving memory of Steven Victor Jakuboski and Darryl Neil Zoerb.

Contents

Foreword

by Constance Wu

"You're watching yourself," he said.

It was his only note.

I'd just finished performing a monologue in my first private coaching session with Craig Archibald. To be honest, I hadn't been expecting much from him. I was a classically trained New York theater actor who'd recently moved to Los Angeles. New York actors are often snobby about LA upon arrival, and I'll admit that I was no exception. None of the other renowned LA acting coaches I'd tried had really clicked. I assumed that Craig would be the same or maybe even worse—because he wasn't even one of the famous LA "gurus." In fact, I'd found him purely by chance. In one of my lazier moments, his name had come up on a quick internet search for acting coaches via zip code. He was the closest to my apartment. If he sucks like all the others, I thought, at least I didn't have to sit in traffic too long.

As a way of getting to know each other, he'd asked me to prepare a scene or monologue. I'd chosen to play "Hannah" from Tennessee Williams's *Night of the Iguana*. I thought I'd done great—language, sense memory, character history, personalization, even tears. Everything that a conservatory-trained actor thought she should be. I felt good, proud. But I was so used to acting teachers trying to prove themselves and impress me with their notes, so I expected some criticism. But something about Craig's note felt different. You're watching yourself. It pinched a nerve inside of me, almost made me angry.

Because, with those three simple words, he'd cut to the heart of the matter. The stuff that classical training, New York snobbery, hard work, IMDb credits, even fame couldn't fake: the truth. He was right. I had been "watching myself." Rather than using my heart to give life to the character, I was using the character to impress Craig with my acting. It had become about my performance, my actor ego. But what about the human being I was portraying? What of Hannah?

At our best, we actors are selfless—giving ourselves over to the character. But at our worst, this selflessness can sour, crossing the line into the worst stereotypes of an actor: vanity, self-absorption, ego. It's hard to recognize this line because ego is so easily disguised: as dedication, righteousness, even humbleness can become its own type of vanity. That's why I needed someone like Craig. Someone who would keep me paying attention, keep making me open my heart. You have to stay diligent in the craft or your work can become quite static and contrived. I've been working steadily for almost a decade, yet I still struggle sometimes.

I remember calling him in a panic one night after the second day of filming on a movie I was starring in. "My instrument shut down," I hyperventilated, breathless with confusion. "I don't know what happened today! Yesterday I was so good!"

Usually, when the work is going well, my heart is open and free and full of surprises. It's a feeling both scary and exhilarating. It's a zone you can't force because it needs freedom and faith and play. I'd been in that zone on my previous "good" day, but the next day my heart had shut down and I'd been unable to connect emotionally to my character. I didn't understand. How had it changed so quickly?

Because on that first day—I hadn't been "watching myself" on set, but I sure as hell had been replaying my performance in my head on the way home. And that's when I crossed the line. Rather than doing right by the character I was playing I had been basking in my own success. And that's why my heart, with its own damn subconscious insurance plan, shut the fuck down, not letting me connect the next day. As if it were saying: Nope, I'm not letting you use me for that. Not letting you use me for your ego.

And that's how I ended up on the phone with Craig, confused and upset and feeling like the Worst Actor in the World.

Craig immediately activated: "Don't panic. This happens," he assured me. "Here's what you need to do. Turn off your phone. Relax and go engage with art that isn't acting related," he said. "Go to an art gallery. Or listen to classical music. Don't think about acting."

I hung up the phone and turned it off. Poured myself a glass of wine, turned on some Mozart, got some colored pencils and paper. Outside my window it was dark, and I looked at the apartment building across from mine. The windows of yellow light and the silhouetted people within—families, couples, people alone. I began to draw them. Wild, juvenile portraits, scribbling with abandon. The Mozart and wine buzzing in my body, I began to wonder what their lives were like. How had their days been? Were they lonely? Instead of worrying about myself and my own performance, I went to bed thinking about the people in the building across the way. The next day, my heart was open again.

See, on that phone call, Craig knew I'd crossed that tremulous line into ego. But rather than teaching me that lesson for the millionth time, he coached me—meeting me where I was, giving me not lessons but tools for the present moment. It wasn't about him and his teachings, it was about helping me.

Craig often says to his actors, "Make it about the other person." It's a Meisner-esque strategy he uses to improve an actor's listening in a scene. But in a larger sense, Craig's instruction to make it about the other person also means serving humanity. That's why Craig includes purpose as part of his actor's philosophy. It's a generous, holistic approach. I've seen him apply this in the way he coaches too. Without judgment and without pride, he unearths an actor's specific obstacles and meets them where they are.

It's been more than ten years since that first coaching session with Craig. When I first met him, I was a struggling actor waiting tables to make ends meet. I had lost faith in myself and hadn't booked a job in more than a year. Within a year of working with him, my work deepened in a way that was fulfilling even without booking a job. Shortly after that, I became a full-time working actor. And today, I've now acted in more than one hundred episodes of television, starred in movies, and been nominated for awards. But that was never the goal. For those of us at the Archibald Studio, success isn't fulfilled with an acting job or an academy award or a paycheck. It's in the present moment—in his living room, sitting in the pink chair, where acting isn't a job, but a vocation. Craig has been with me through all of it. On days of dark despair, he helped me find the strength to pull myself back up. And when I'd sometimes get lost in the manic highs of success, his acting class reminded me how being on the ground felt so much better than being in the air.

I still go to Craig's group classes when I'm not working. I joke and call it my church but, jokes aside, I have often considered religion and art to have parallels. Like church, Craig's classes are a community of practitioners who hold a reverence for the mysteries and wonder of the human experience. Who search for meaning in the present moment. Who practice faithfully. Who often falter and fall into ego and fear and righteousness not because of the faith's flaws, but because we are humans practicing imperfectly.

And how much fun it is to explore, to constantly be practicing, to never be perfect! How joyful the discovery of it is! He and I spend a lot of our private coaching sessions giddy with excitement: "Ooooh, that's so rich!" we squeal when we discover a great character history possibility or, "Hmmm that doesn't fit right, why doesn't that pinch me inside?" I say, when my gut doesn't twinge, and we hunker down to brainstorm for something else. When either of us sees a great performance, we call each other and get so excited, practically pumping our fists in the air—and can talk about it for hours. Craig used to be a New York theater guy too, so we can geek out together over the brilliance of Tennessee Williams or August Wilson. He is my coach and my friend. My kindred spirit. I feel so grateful and lucky to have found him. I think you will too.

On the red carpet with Constance Wu at the 2016 Emmy Awards.

Preface

This book is for the storytellers of the world. It addresses the art of acting, but its principles weave through the performing arts, and I gladly welcome all artists interested in my take on the craft, discipline, and business of acting. Perhaps you will find applications to your life and art that prove helpful; nothing would please me more.

This book is also for the family and friends of actors. Often, the journey that actors embark upon seems so foreign and treacherous that family and friends feel deep concern for an actor/loved one's well-being. (I know. I've been there. We love you for that!)

I hope this book will help you understand why the actor in your life has committed to an art and industry that is so difficult and yet so ultimately soul-fulfilling and life-rewarding.

Finally, and most obviously, this book is for actors. I will share with you the knowledge I've gained in my several decades in the profession as an actor, coach, writer, director, and producer. I hope I can help you on your journey.

I wrote this book because I wish I'd had someone like me to talk to when I started in the industry, someone I could trust to tell me the truth and do it kindly. I didn't have that person. I had to learn it the hard way.

There is a purple haze of nonsense around our work as actors, a miasma of rumor, gossip, and fantasy. Much of it is counterproductive. Little of it is wise or helpful. I have experienced my full share and I want no more of it.

I've been an acting coach since 1995. Many of my clients have countless years of experience, which has given me a broad perspective. I have witnessed nearly every possibility of success and failure, bliss and disappointment, joy and heartbreak.

In offering you what I believe to be the truth about both the art of acting and the broader film and television industry, I aim to give you clarity; to simplify your focus; and to help you achieve your goals faster and more easily so that you can succeed sooner and use that success to help our world become a better place—nothing less!

As an actor, you're part of a grand storytelling tradition. Storytellers entertain, educate, heal, and inspire. The stories we tell each other teach empathy, expand horizons, and help us understand different points of view. We mirror life, so that the world sees itself and gains new perspectives. In making audiences laugh, cry, and feel deeply, we heal with laughter and love, with the recognition that others also suffer and rejoice.

This industry can be particularly challenging, which makes it easy to adopt a "victim" mindset. I see this every day as I coach actors at the Archibald Studio in Los Angeles. I battle this tendency toward self-pity with a simple but powerful dictum: Make everything make you better. If you can use every difficulty as an inspiration to self-betterment, you change your mindset from victim to champion.

Refuse to be a victim or to bemoan your plight (easy as it may be after yet another audition, another brusque dismissal, or another empty morning spent waiting for a callback). Make everything make you better. I've done it, I've taught it, I've seen it in action. It works.

Actors have a special function in society. We have a special place in the vast tradition of storytellers. Storytelling is crucial to the advancement of society. Throughout history, storytellers have inspired humankind forward and onward to be the best we can be.

In my opinion, succeeding as an actor means tapping into your authentic self, speaking your unique truth, and telling your singular story. In doing so, by tiny increments, you help to make our world a better place. Because life is difficult and wonderful, and there's always a new war to fight, a newborn to celebrate, or a newsworthy catastrophe to recover from, the world needs you to succeed.

Who I Am

As a kid growing up on the Canadian prairies in Saskatoon, Saskatchewan, I always wanted to be an actor. In my first role, at age four, I was Peter Rabbit.

I also had a real aptitude for dance. It was a natural part of my self-expression. I loved ballet, jazz, and tap. Though I focused on becoming an actor, my preferred workout came from dance.

I was good. Really good. The best boy in class. The best in school. Teachers would tell me how talented I was. In my fabulous imaginary world, I was a celebrated world-class actor and dancer. I'd daydream about all the acting/dancing roles I'd land. Move over, Gene Kelly and Donald O'Connor, here comes Craig Archibald!

Enjoying one of my favorite classes at the Neighborhood Playhouse, New York City, 1988.

In 1989, I auditioned for my first Broadway show. I can't even recall what show it was—some new musical doing a trial run in a remote New Jersey theater before returning to New York for what everyone hoped would be a long run. Perfect. I would establish myself quickly and land on the Great White Way!

I showed up bright and early at one of the big Broadway theaters for the open dance call. It was like the opening scene of Bob Fosse's film *All That Jazz*—hundreds of young dancers were preparing to audition. I was in heaven and hoped to be good enough to be invited back to the acting call the next day.

I was given my number, 21, and guided to the holding area where all the Broadway Brats of 1989 were preparing. Then came my first moment of doubt: the warm-up stretches! I was in sweatpants and sneakers. These guys were serious professionals. Lycra body suits! Leg warmers! Capezio Jazz shoes! Effortless splits. Plying their bodies into stretches that made my testicles retract. Oh, and the acrobatic warm-ups! The handstands! The flips! The round offs! I daintily rolled my ankles in the corner, avoiding eye contact.

With faltering bravado, I marched onto the enormous stage with my group of dancers. Out in the cavernous house was a long table with lights, and behind it the creative team: the director, the writer, the lyricist, the composer, the company stage manager, a few producers, and, most importantly for me, the choreographer.

The dance captain corralled us and began to call out the dance steps for the audition piece, "To the left—glissade, assemble, jete—" I'd been dance training for more than ten years, but at this moment I was nervous and tense. All I heard was "Gleeblah, ablahblah, jeblee, blah blarq!"

I was way out of my league and in deep trouble. I eased my way back through the crowd of dancers, desperately searching for an exit door. There was none to be found.

"Here we go, one rehearsal!" the dance captain barked. "A five, six, seven, eight!"

En masse, following his direction, the dancers moved to the left. Then the turn to the right, and the group danced back across the stage. I tried to follow and learn the moves, but it was all too fast, too difficult. Thirty-two beats: sixteen to the left, sixteen to the right, and finished.

"OK, here we go!" the suddenly terrifying dance captain announced. "Let me see numbers 1, 2, and 3. Number 1 downstage left. Number 2 upstage center. And number 3 downstage right." On cue, three of the Broadway Boys moved into position. With a brief count in, they were off—dancing brilliantly, nailing the jumps, turns, and kicks.

The rest of us pooled upstage, flattening into a semicircle against the back wall, watching. Again, I searched for an exit. Nothing. The only way out was through. Years of class, sweat, and tears bubbled up in my heart. I bucked up and tried valiantly to learn the steps by watching.

On we went. "Numbers 4, 5, and 6." Smart asses added triple turns when only two were necessary. "Numbers 7, 8, and 9." I focused with the concentration of a cornered cobra.

Finally, the dreaded moment: "Numbers 19, 20, and 21."

Mind frozen, blood boiling, back solid as a rope, I took my place downstage right and looked out at that huge, beautiful Broadway house with the runway of creators behind the table. This was the moment I'd worked so hard for. And I was completely unprepared. A brief countdown—"a five, six, seven, eight"—and we were off!

I did my best: to the left, stumbling, bumbling, and then to the right, again stretching, reaching, and failing miserably. The music ended. There was not a sound. Just a pure and complete silence, as in deep outer space. It was over; my failure was a colossal and remarkable occasion my enemies would have enjoyed with glee.

Humbled and humiliated, I turned to exit off stage right when I heard the dance captain call out, "Numbers 22, 23, and 21!"

Wait! What? I turned to the dance captain. He positioned me in the upstage center spot and looked me in the eye: "You're going to do it until you get it right, kid."

My heart sank. Despair. Humiliation.

And so on we danced. Numbers 24, 25, and 21. . . . Numbers 37, 38, and 21. . . . Eventually, in the high fifties, I nailed the dance. There was a condescending smattering of applause from the high-bottomed boys.

The dance captain said, "You may leave."

"And you may kiss my ass," I thought as I exited stage right.

Offstage, I mopped the sweat from my face with my T-shirt and tried to calm myself.

I was approached by an assistant stage manager named Todd. "They want to see you at the table."

Who? The creative team?

I followed him out into the dark, air-conditioned theater. On the stage, the dancing boys continued. No one else was being made to "do it until you do it right, kid." As we approached the table, I could see the faces of the creative team behind the lights. They were all smiles.

"Oh my god," the director said with a big grin. "What is your name?"

"Craig Archibald," I answered breathlessly.

"That was fantastic! You are very brave, Mr. Archibald!"

"Thank you. . . . I'm sorry I wasn't. . . ."

"No, no, no. We need brave boys like you! Can you act?"

"Yes, sir," I replied.

"Did you study?"

"Yes, sir, at the Neighborhood Playhouse."

"With Sandy Meisner?"

"Yes, sir."

"Good, well, OK Craig Archibald, we'll be seeing people tomorrow for the acting roles. Todd will give you the sides to prepare. We look forward to seeing your work."

I could barely believe my ears. The gods had been generous.

"Thank you, sir. Thank you."

As Todd led me away, the choreographer spoke up, "Are you sure you can act?"

I turned and looked at him, at all of them, and replied with my biggest Broadway grin: "You bet!"

"Thank Christ," the choreographer replied, "because you sure as shit can't dance!"

Fuck it. "So long, Fred Astaire. Hello, Marlon Brando."

PART I
THE CRAFT

1
Your Journey

I love actors. I love our art form. I celebrate the remarkable bravery it takes to choose this business as a profession. I salute your commitment. I believe in you. I am on your side.

When you work with me at the Archibald Studio, we begin by looking at your foundation, both as an actor and as an entrepreneur. Without a proper foundation, on what will you build an enduring career? In Hollywood, the earth quakes—in more ways than one. You might be the smartest kid in Albuquerque or the standout in your college acting class, but Hollywood doesn't care. Here, you're just another wannabe.

Take time to self-investigate. Keep a journal. Use therapy as a means of self-exploration. Think about your art, your method, your business, and your life. Take the tools I offer you and work on yourself. If you really want to succeed, you need to be your best self. You need to focus and work hard. It's a long road.

As Sanford Meisner said, "It takes twenty years to become an artist." He explained that the first ten years are spent in the technical study of the art, mastering the techniques and methods of your art form. The second ten years are spent in the mastery of the craft of your work. Finally, after twenty years of diligence, you'll be so deeply connected to your work that you won't need to think about technique or craft—your art will simply flow.

It is also imperative that you check your foundation as a businessperson. This may sound scary to you; it does to many artists. But if you want to succeed, you must become an entrepreneur. You own a business, which provides a service called acting, in a marketplace called Hollywood. Because many other entrepreneurs provide the same service, you must make certain that yours is the best it can be.

Ultimately, your goal is to grow a small business into a large one. It starts with understanding that you need to be wise about the industry in which you operate. You must provide such a unique and valuable service that there will be no doubt of your success.

I have no interest in being your guru. I'm your coach. You are not my student; you are my client. It's an important distinction. Smart business people hire smart advisers.

One of the best parts of being an entrepreneur is this: The people in your life who do not understand what being an actor entails, or why you would choose to celebrate your talent for storytelling, usually do understand and respect entrepreneurship. So the next time you have a difficult conversation with your father, mother, grandparent, or best friend who thinks you're being silly, stupid, or self-indulgent, just tell them you're an entrepreneur in show business!

An important lesson that every young actor must learn is this: You are enough as you are. I mentioned the purple haze of nonsense around acting. The images we receive from movies, television, magazines, and social media suggest that you have to strive to attain a type of physical perfection. That you have to be sexy. Or cool.

Not so. Yes, you need to be healthy. Yes, you need to be in good shape. Yes, you need to constantly seek to be your best. But in doing so, don't forget that the most important part of you is not your cheekbones or skin tone. The most important part of you is your heart. That's your most valuable asset.

Do not attempt to be like other actors. Celebrate your individuality. Bring your unique soul to the work. Often, it's one's essence, one's spirit, that makes the difference between who gets a job and who doesn't.

This is not an invitation to be silly. Performing and sensationalizing an idea of quirky or sexy or cool is off-putting. Simply be yourself and be professional. As I say in class, "The wrapping may be as pretty as you like, but the present is what's inside the box."

Remember, at the end of the day, that you are a storyteller. In successful storytelling, there is a crucial moment called the catharsis. The climax. The release of powerful, suppressed emotion. It's the moment when the audience members fully click with the material—they have a personal, deeply intimate response to the work.

Have you seen *E. T. the Extra-Terrestrial*? All of director Steven Spielberg's elements of filmmaking work beautifully toward the catharsis. When the magic of E.T. lifts the boys on the bikes to help them escape, it is a remarkable moment—the actors, the art direction, the music, and the audience's suspended disbelief all come together to create a magnificent emotional release.

Catharsis is achieved only if the audience believes the character to be so real that they're willing to suspend their disbelief and actively invest in the character. On one level, they know they're watching a movie, sure; but if they believe the actors implicitly, they suspend that disbelief. If they trust the actors, the piece will do what it is intended to do: entertain, educate, heal, and inspire the audience. When that magic happens, the artist has succeeded.

Victim or Champion?

You have a fundamental choice in life. You can be a victim or a champion. I insist that my clients choose champion. It isn't always easy. Negative thoughts can overwhelm a peaceful mind, especially in our increasingly erratic and uncertain world, but mastery of your mind is the secret to happiness. Seek to understand how you truly function, not how others do. Commit to investigating yourself. Commit to your own personal journey of champion.

"The Hero's Journey" is a literary plot device scholar Joseph Campbell writes about in his 1947 book *The Hero with a Thousand Faces*. This classic structure is used in countless television dramas and comedy scripts (and plays and novels and epic poems and even television commercials). It has deep roots in myth and spiritual ritual, Campbell's fields of expertise.

The hero (or heroine) goes through several stages of growth by facing tremendous challenges and, in doing so, grows to become more than they ever imagined they could be—they conquer a foreign or perceived evil, they achieve an almost impossible physical feat, and they not only save themselves and others but also teach their family and/or society a great moral lesson.

If you analyze the plot of almost any classic film or television series, you will find the hero's journey. Luke Skywalker, Hermione Granger, Wonder Woman, Batman, even Peter Griffin and Lucy Ricardo—all are built on the structure of the hero's journey. Homer's *Odyssey* is an epic hero's journey. So also, structurally at least, is a thirty-second television spot in which the hero, a bumbling gardener, overcomes his ugly-lawn obstacle by taking his neighbor's advice and applying fertilizer.

Joseph Campbell broke the hero's journey down into seventeen stages. Hollywood development executive Christopher Vogler shortened it to twelve easy-to-understand steps in his book *The Writer's Journey: Mythic Structure for Writers*. I highly recommend both books, and not just to writers. When you work as an actor, you need to understand basic writing principles as well.

My version of the journey has you, the actor, as hero. You set out on a quest and overcome every obstacle. I am addressing here your psychological development as well as your passage through the world, and the tremendous reward you receive when you live your life as a hero's journey.

This journey is difficult. Remember, you are attempting to be extraordinary. You will have challenges. You will have to make sacrifices.

Becoming a successful actor is as difficult as becoming an Olympic athlete. You must think this way. You must bring the same discipline and focus. If you don't, someone else will. And chances are they will book the job and you won't.

I have great respect for anyone trying to answer their hero's journey call. I encourage you to fight and dream and scrape your way toward your goal. I can guarantee you a remarkable life. It may not always be pretty, it may not be luxurious, and it may not end with a star on the Hollywood Walk of Fame. But it will be a wonderfully satisfying journey, and uniquely yours.

I encourage my clients to find heroes' journeys that inspire them—others who have faced tragedy or misfortune and turned great challenges into great successes. The world is full of extraordinary people who have been thrust into terrible difficulties due to natural catastrophes, wars, accidents, or simple bad luck. Their stories of persevering, of battling back—from near-death to survival, from ignominy to glory, from long shot to champion—can be awe-inspiring.

Collect hero stories of your own. You are surrounded by heroes and heroines. Keep your eyes open and you will find inspiration closer than you realize, perhaps from a family member battling terminal illness, a friend who invests all their money in a startup, even a local homeless person who's been through more difficulty than you can imagine. One of my favorite actors, Chris Cooper, sadly lost his son at age seventeen. Another talented actor, Julia Louis-Dreyfus, fought through a terrifying bout of breast cancer. Heroes are everywhere.

One of my personal heroes is my cousin, Murray. He was in a horrific car/train accident in his youth. Both his sister Patsy and his brother Charlie were killed. Murray survived and made a beautiful life for himself. His journey, through a terrible ordeal to a life of honor and integrity, makes him one of the great heroes of my life.

Joseph Campbell tells us that in every hero's journey, a guide appears to help the hero find their way to their unique and individual goal. I like to think of myself as the lucky guide who gets to help my heroes on their journeys. Thank you for trusting me with your work. This book is meant to help you on your hero's journey, to discover ways of encountering and surmounting every challenge, no matter how formidable, on your path toward a successful acting career.

2
The Method

Often misunderstood, often confused, the Stanislavski System stands at the center of American (some would say global) approaches to the craft of acting.

For ease of explanation, *the Method* is the Americanized branding of the "Stanislavski System." For the purposes of this book, we will use *the Method* to mean *the Stanislavski System that became the American Method*.

Many young actors don't know the history of the Method or confuse it with nonsense. If you're going to be the best artist you can be, and you plan to be the best entrepreneur you can be, you need to know the history and evolution of your field.

In the early 1900s, the Moscow Arts Theater was one of the premier theater companies in Russia. The artistic director was a man named Konstantin Stanislavski.

At the time, the style of performance was presentational—what we would call "forced," "mechanical," or "over" acting. (The opposite is "representational" acting, which is realistically bound to the actor's truthful embodiment of the character's circumstances.)

The actors wore heavy makeup and extravagant costumes. They had tremendous vocal capacity, because they had to tell the story in spacious auditoriums or—an even greater challenge—outdoors. This was before microphones and audio systems, at a time when an audience, if they did not like your performance, would throw fruits and vegetables at you! (There are some days I wish we could still do that!)

There are many accounts of the influences that affected Stanislavski and his approach to acting. One such influence was the French actor Benoit-Constant

Coquelin, and the French psychologist Theodule Ribot articulated the emotional and imaginative relevance of the Method in his "Essay on the Creative Imagination" (1900) and his 1903 book *The Psychology of Emotions.*

Whatever the Method's wellsprings, Stanislavski envisioned a new kind of performance—a subtle and intricate display of true human behavior that would infuse the character and make the audience see him or her as an authentic being. The members of the Moscow Arts Theater spent some ten years perfecting this approach.

The troupe's work made them popular in Moscow. Word spread across Europe about a wonderful theater company doing brilliantly personal work that was deeply connected to the heart of the writing and to the truth of the characters' experience within the play. As actors and theater professionals came to watch and study, the Method began to spread.

In time, the Moscow Arts Theater Company became so famous that they toured. At one point, they came to America. Unfortunately, the plays were performed in Russian, and American audiences simply weren't interested in a group of Russians emoting heavily in small theaters while speaking a foreign language! It would take thirty years for the Method to finally assimilate into the American theater and film acting process.

The man credited with bringing the Method to America was an actor named Richard Boleslavsky. A member of Stanislavski's company, he was forced to leave Moscow during the Russian Revolution in 1917 and return to his home country, Poland. There, a friend introduced him to a movie camera. It was a critical moment in the history of film acting. Boleslavsky combined the film camera and the Method to create a beautiful new approach to on-camera acting.

The ravages of the First World War forced Boleslavsky and his family to flee Poland and move to New York City. There, on the Lower East Side, he and his wife created the American Laboratory Theatre, where he taught the Stanislavski Method to young actors in the 1920s.

While teaching in New York, Boleslavsky also began a career as a movie director. His films were the first to have actors use the Method. The quality of the acting caught the eye of Hollywood, and Boleslavsky eventually moved to Los Angeles, where he directed many films in the 1930s. He died of a heart attack on a soundstage at MGM in Hollywood, an unfortunately abrupt ending, but how's that for a hero's journey!

At the American Laboratory Theatre in New York, one of Boleslavsky's students was a young actor named Lee Strasberg. Strasberg, along with Cheryl Crawford and a theater director named Harold Clurman, founded the Group Theatre, the first American theater company to adopt the Stanislavski Method.

The Group Theatre became the preeminent New York City theater company in the 1930s. Their critical success was remarkable; for the first time, American audiences saw actors truly crying, truly laughing, and truly working from their wonderful, vulnerable souls.

Acting would never be the same.

After the Group Theater disbanded in the early 1940s, actors from the company continued to work in theater and film. Some created theater schools and taught the Method. Those schools included the Neighborhood Playhouse (led by Sanford Meisner), the HB Studio (started by Uta Hagen and Herbert Berghof), the Stella Adler Conservatory (started by Stella Adler), and the Actors Studio (started by Group Theater members Cheryl Crawford, Bobby Lewis, and Elia Kazan). Bobby Lewis went on to teach at the Yale School of Drama. Lee Strasberg taught at the Actors Studio until his death in 1982.

These institutions widely introduced Stanislavski's Method to American actors. The movie stars who emerged from those schools are a Hollywood who's who: Montgomery Clift, Marlon Brando, Shelley Winters, Kim Hunter, Gregory Peck, Eva Marie Saint, Paul Newman, Patricia Neal, Robert Duvall, Robert DeNiro, and many, many more. And not just actors, but many writers and directors as well.

Some of the actors became teachers. All of them used the Method in their approach to the work. Each actor/teacher emphasized the different elements of the Method that made their own work better.

Lee Strasberg had a particularly powerful influence through his tutelage at the Actors Studio. There, the term *the Method* found its footing and took over as the popular American idiom from *the Stanislavski System*.

The original Stanislavski System differs from the Strasberg Method in one major way. It focuses on the motivating action of the character, the "why" behind the character's behavior. Stanislavski's actor must "do something." Only then does the dramatic situation result in feelings from the character/actor.

The Strasberg Method focuses on the emotions that harmonize with the character's experience inside the dramatic situation. Strasberg focused on the feeling or emotion inside the experience prior to the motivation. Strasberg's actor must "feel something."

This may sound like splitting hairs, but the differing results can be profound.

Mr. Stanislavski's approach works best for me, personally, as an actor, but I keep all roads open for my clients to find the access point that best serves their work.

Over time, the Method has undergone many subtle variations. Innumerable teachers, coaches, and actors have interpreted the work of Stanislavski and his company, which has sometimes created misinformation and confusion. Because of this, some actors are mocked for the deep personal work it takes to connect to the truth of the characters they're portraying.

But the Method has also led to deeply beautiful work. Watching James Dean in *East of Eden*, or Meryl Streep in *Sophie's Choice*, or Sean Penn in *Milk*, you can sense an artist connecting their own deep human reality to the deep human truth of the character. This is what Sandy Meisner called "living truthfully under imaginary circumstances."

The Method has also created what I call (if you'll forgive me) "actorbating." There's nothing more tedious than watching someone actorbate for the camera. Look how much I can feel! Look how adept I am at being emotional! Method acting elicits many different responses from audiences, who may find one particular artist's work brilliant and moving but another's irritating and self-indulgent.

I believe that almost every actor working in America today, indeed in the world, has been affected by Stanislavski. Even those who are "anti-Method" are reacting to the influences that Stanislavski discovered. Playwright David Mamet, for example, urges actors to "just say the lines," although I believe that goes against the integrity of our work.

This is where some young actors get confused: It seems there are many different Methods. Maybe, but they all grow out of Stanislavski's work with the Moscow Arts Theatre. They all introduce the young actor to the essence of the work, which is:

- Know and understand yourself thoroughly.
- Gain a complete, vulnerable accessibility to your emotional life.
- Use your heart and soul in the creation of the characters you play as you live truthfully under the imaginary circumstances of the script.

It is your job as an actor to discover how the Method works best for you. No one can tell you exactly how that will be. Every artist has an individual response. Any teacher or coach who is didactic or dogmatic about the process is making a mistake.

You must find for yourself the best way to stimulate and access your emotional life so that your performances are grounded in a vulnerable truth and you never find yourself faking it—never end up "acting." As Stanislavski said, "Create your own method. Don't depend slavishly on mine. Make up something that will work for you!"

This isn't good advice only for the young actor. The work never ends. One never truly masters the Method (or any art form, for that matter), because the work relies on your organically truthful humanity, and because you are constantly growing, so too must your process. It's a lifelong challenge to remain in top technical form. The great actors of all ages, all through their careers, work constantly on their craft, pushing themselves to find their authentic, organic truth. The work is never over. That's part of the joy of being an artist!

I've had the good fortune of meeting many of my heroes over the years, including Al Pacino. He sometimes shared with me his inspirations. Over dinner one night, he said, "Craig, I've just discovered Google Images! It's amazing! I punch something in, hit Search, and hours of homework are done for me!" Here he was, a brilliant actor, now in his seventies, delighted to find new things to help him become better.

How the Method Works

Due to poor translations and the Soviet government editing, Stanislavski's first editions in English—*An Actor Prepares*, *Building a Character*, and *My Life in Art*—make for difficult reading. In 2008, Jean Benedetti went back to the original Russian texts and reinterpreted Stanislavski's work in two books I highly recommend: *An Actor's Work* and *An Actor's Work on a Role*. Please read those books. (Remember, though, that Stanislavski wrote about acting on stage. That's why the books can at times be more "theatrical" than "cinematic.")

How, exactly, does the Method work? There are enough books to fill a library seeking to answer that question, but I've boiled it down to the following visual showing how you connect to the emotional life of the character. That connection is the cornerstone of all Method work.

Read clockwise from 1 to 8, below.

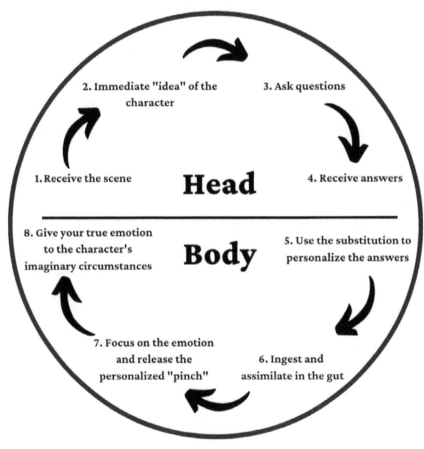

How the Method works.

Number 1. You're Ready to Receive the Scene.

You're handed a script, which includes your role. Let's take *Romeo and Juliet* and choose a scene we all recognize, the balcony scene. Ladies: you are given the role of Juliet. Gentlemen: you'll be playing Romeo.

Number 2. You Read the Scene and Get an Immediate Idea of the Character.

You can almost see them, can't you? She's a pretty young girl of thirteen, in her nightgown, on her balcony, looking up at the moon and saying, "O Romeo, Romeo, wherefore art thou Romeo?" He's a handsome, slightly older lad, stealing over the wall, looking up at her window and saying, "But soft! What light through yonder window breaks?"

If you're a fan of Baz Luhrmann's 1996 film, you might imagine Claire Danes as Juliet. Romeo might look like Leonardo DiCaprio. Or perhaps your imagination evokes the beauties from the Franco Zeffirelli film version of 1968.

This immediate idea of the character is not wrong. We all get a similar image, particularly when it's a famous character. But the immediate idea is just a starting point; it's not developed or processed to a deeper place.

Now, many actors simply work from this immediate idea. They play directly from it. They can play a thug perfectly, they believe, because they know what a "thug" is. They see the idea in their head, so they play that image. Or they play "the stern judge." Or "the efficient nurse."

They're playing these roles from a cerebral, immediate idea place. They're not interrogating the character, not doing deep homework. They have the right "look" for the role, they learn the lines, they go in front of the camera and do simple work from an uninvestigated idea.

Sometimes it works. When we see the TV show or movie, and they're the banker or thug or nurse, we accept them in the role, but they have no impact on us whatsoever. We don't remember them, don't care about them. We don't wonder who they are or what happened to them. They're simply lost in the vacuum of bad acting. It's bad acting because they're embodying not a nuanced character but an immediate idea.

An idea is not what you work from in the Method. You don't act from your head. You act from your heart and gut. You want to be emotionally superior, not intellectually superior. This is a major difference, by the way, from most other professional endeavors. Your whole life, people have told you to be smart. My instruction is "be heart." Let someone else be head-smart; you be heart-smart. Heart-smart is art-smart.

Your goal in the Method is to live truthfully under imaginary circumstances. To be truthful in your acting work, you have to be smart intellectually, but it's also important to be smart emotionally. Your emotional quotient (EQ) is more important than your intellectual quotient (IQ). Daniel Goleman popularized EQ in his book *Emotional Intelligence*, and it made us reconsider what "smart" really means.

Many storytellers struggled in school, where the IQ is celebrated. Many people connect to life on the deeper EQ. It's not a concept that's universally celebrated within the halls of education, but you must employ it in your work as an actor.

How does this work? You let your original idea of the character land. You acknowledge it. "OK, that's my immediate idea of who Juliet/Romeo is." But then you must dig deeper to get an understanding of who your character truly is.

Number 3. Ask Questions.

Investigate the imaginary circumstances. These are simple questions: "Who is Juliet?" "What does Romeo want in this scene?" "What is her motivation?"

"What is his obstacle?" Questions about their lives, the ones you ask when you meet someone. "What's your background?" "Who are your parents?" "Where did you grow up?"

Number 4. From Those Questions, We Get Answers and Begin to Form a Fuller Picture of This Character.

We get a much richer picture than we had in the immediate idea. Our image becomes more nuanced and complex. We understand them much better. We now have a richer, deeper understanding of who the character is. But it's still a brainy understanding.

Many actors work from this brainy idea, this intellectual grasp. These are sneaky actors. We can see how smart they are. They've answered the questions and they know what they're doing. They're answer-driven. And we can sometimes appreciate them (we can really want to like them, anyway). In the end, though, they leave us feeling a bit cold.

These are the actors you watch and don't like and don't quite know why. You can see they're acting a part well. But you don't connect to them emotionally, don't believe the character, and ultimately don't respond deeply to the performance. We don't connect to them emotionally because they aren't connected emotionally. They're connected intellectually, and so we have an intellectual response.

As we've seen, storytelling becomes powerful when the story affects the audience in a deeply emotional way. The catharsis is then forceful and the work successful.

As a Method actor, you don't stop with answers, because that is not the work that brings the deepest result. You take it further. You make a commitment to the answered question that brings a deeply emotional connection.

You take the answer and connect to it personally; you ingest it into your gut. You're creating an emotional pinch. You must be connected emotionally and then live truthfully in the moment from that emotionally connected place.

Number 5. To Ingest the Answer, Use a substitution (Also Referred to as an "As If").

What is a substitution and how does it work? You substitute a personal experience for the character's experience. You use your own unique experience of life to bring the character to life. And because each artist is unique, no two performances of the same part could ever be the same. Nor should you ever want to do a performance that mimics the performance of another actor.

There are three fundamental ways to do a substitution:

1. You can go into your past and use your memory to connect to the answer.
2. You can use your present circumstances to connect to the answer.
3. You can go into the future and use your imagination to connect to the answer.

If you asked Juliet, "What are you doing in this scene?" she might realize, "I'm grasping my personal power for the first time in my life. I'm becoming my own woman." Now, as luck and good writing would have it, Shakespeare made the answer to "What are you doing in this scene, Romeo?" similar to Juliet's. Romeo, too, is grasping his personal power for the first time, becoming his own man. That's part of the glory of the scene—two young people becoming their independent selves together.

After arriving at the answer—"I am grasping my personal power for the first time and becoming my own woman/man"—you can connect with the character's circumstances by doing a substitution—"This is as if I'm grasping my personal power for the first time and becoming my own person."

Go into your past and recall a time when you stepped into becoming your own person. Maybe you stood up to a schoolyard bully for the first time. Maybe you defied your parents. Maybe you called bullshit on a manipulative boss. Revisit the circumstances of that event, use your memory, and your sense memory, to fully work up the emotional values you felt at the time.

Or use a self-empowering moment in your present life—a personal breakthrough in acting class, perhaps—to work up your emotional pinch.

Or imagine an event that would equal the value of the event in the character's life—a situation so fully imagined that you have a genuine emotional reaction. A moment when you'd be grasping your personal power.

Some coaches believe you should only use one of these substitution options. Stanislavski suggested using all three time periods (past, present, future), then stepping back and assessing which pinched you the hardest emotionally. Focus on that event so intensely that you actually feel it in the pit of your stomach.

Also, you can use many other inspirations to pinch your emotions, such as photos, music, art, or poetry. A sunset could do it. Anything that makes you feel the desired emotional pinch.

Number 6: You Have Now Successfully Ingested the Answer into Your Gut.

The graphic images and language in substitutions are self-renewing and continually growing. Allow them to change and develop over time.

Number 7: Focus on That Emotion. Feel it. Now Slowly Release Your Substitution.

No longer focus on your own particular emotional pinch but maintain the heavy emotional connection. Simply focus on that golden orb of emotion inside you. Now, you're ready to take the final step.

Number 8: Give That Emotion to the Character.

It's the feeling you're giving to the character, not the actual incident of your substitution. After you focus totally on the feeling, give that golden orb of feeling to the character.

Once you've given the feeling to the character, you can work on the scene by improvising it, talking it aloud, not focusing on the written dialogue, but instead working directly from that truthful, transferred emotion. Now you're living under the imaginary circumstances as if they were truly happening to you, the character.

And remember, we have only answered one question. Layer in many questions and their relevant emotions and you will develop a deeply layered emotional reality. Line memorization comes more easily when you're layering the emotional life into the character and not focusing on repetitious drilling of lines.

The following logic and sequencing of human behavior reflects the same logic and sequencing of the Method:

- In life, we experience reality through our senses. In acting, we are given the specific circumstances from the script.
- In life, our mind processes the information we receive from our senses. We appraise the situation. In acting, our mind has to create the images of the given circumstances using our sense memories, then create the appraisal or point of view of the character.

- In life, the appraisal creates response reflexes. In acting, the appraisal creates response reflexes.
- In life, feelings are the result of those responses. In acting, feelings are the result of those responses.
- In life, action is taken in response to those feelings. In acting, the inner and outer actions of the character are a response to those feelings.
- In life, we have emotional responses to the actions we take. In acting, we have emotional responses to the actions the character takes.
- The logic and sequencing using a script is as follows: The event in the script, along with the given circumstances, gives us mental images.
- We then place an appraisal or perspective on those mental images.
- These appraisals result in a task or action we are inspired to take.
- The doing of that task or action, and the responses to that doing, creates feelings.

The key thing here is that feelings come later. They do not start the process; they're the result of it. This is essential to understanding how the Method works. Too often, actors try to cry. Or laugh. This is backward. Tears and giggles are not an impetus but a result.

This fundamental sequence is the natural way all humans react to stimuli. The beauty of the Method is that it is based on nature. The natural process becomes your process.

Have you seen Viola Davis's Oscar-winning performance as Rose Maxson in the 2017 film *Fences*? It's an outstanding display of her capacity to connect to her own emotional truth and infuse it in her character to bring that character vividly to life. British actor Josh O'Connor's work in another 2017 film, *God's Own Country*, is another example of an actor's terrific interconnectedness between the soul and the role.

My Own Breakthrough

As I said, I grew up in western Canada, in a lovely little city called Saskatoon, Saskatchewan. This is farm country. These are God-fearing, God-loving, tough-as-nails folk. Saskatchewan has proudly created many world-class ice hockey players—tough boys. Growing up in that culture, it was unacceptable for a young man to show any kind of vulnerability in public. Boys did not cry.

Between 1975 and 1984, I performed in more than eighty plays in my hometown. I have two large scrapbooks of programs and photographs of a busy childhood in the theater. At age fifteen, I turned professional (joining Actors Equity and ACTRA, the Canadian film and television union, equivalent to the Screen Actors Guild in the United States).

After receiving my bachelor of arts in theater from the University of Saskatchewan, I moved to London. There, I studied privately with teachers from the Royal Academy of Dramatic Arts, including Gloria Lytten. I also worked at the Royal National Theatre of Great Britain, under the mentorship of Sir Ian McKellen.

Improvising with comedy and tragedy with my Neighborhood Playhouse buddy, Kevin Stapleton.

In London, I'd go to the movies and watch my heroes—Pacino, DeNiro, Sean Penn, and Eric Roberts—do beautiful, heartfelt, deeply personal work, but I never really understood how they connected to their emotional truth. I'd had lots of stage training but had not studied Stanislavski's Method at all.

In 1987, I moved to New York and studied at the Neighborhood Playhouse, where I learned from the master teachers Sanford Meisner and Robert Xavier Modica.

One day, we were doing a variation of the "repetition exercise," which Meisner invented as a training tool. Members of the class could tap in and jump into a repetition with another member of the class. I was, at that time, rather self-righteous and confident (others might have said egotistical and self-centered). That day, my classmates took turns calling me out on my behavior. It was painful.

I left for a long lunch break in a park near Sutton Place and the East River, feeling sorry for myself, humbled at the recognition of my less-than-exemplary character points.

That afternoon, when I returned to Modica's class, I had a breakthrough. I did a small scene with a fellow actor named Heather Frazier. We set our stakes in the scene high. The buildup of emotional preparation for class, plus the humiliation I'd felt that morning, combined to promote a huge emotional breakthrough. For the first time in my life, I was able to access not just tears, but also shame, rage, and true vulnerability in public. I understood that day something every actor must learn: you must go deep to access the core of your vulnerability.

3
The Archibald Questions

After graduating from the Neighborhood Playhouse, I went on to study with Suzanne Shepherd. I worked hard to establish a professional career, but after several years I found myself at a crossroads. I had an inconsistency problem. One audition I'd be great; the next I'd stink up the room. One night on stage, I would feel wonderful, inspired, alive, connected, and free. The next, I'd feel horrible, self-conscious, emotionally constipated.

I returned to the lessons of my teachers. I reread my notes. I looked at my problems objectively. What I didn't realize for a long time was that I needed to stop trying to do things other people's way. Instead, I needed to look inside myself and figure out, from my training, my own approach to the work.

What I came up with was the following set of questions. I methodically approached the work from the beginning, from the simplest questions to the most complex. I could then assimilate the answers to those questions before giving them to the character. This way my auditions and performances would be consistent and inspired because they'd always be coming from my most vulnerable truth.

I believe every artist has to do this. You must look at the way you work, learn how to pinch yourself, how to protect yourself, how your heart and your brain work, so that you can, in any circumstance, deliver the best work possible.

These questions are not original or unique. They are similar to questions Stanislavski and his entourage worked with back in 1900. (See the final chapter of the Benedetti book *An Actor's Work on a Role* for the twenty-five steps that Stanislavski used.) However, I developed these from my own experience.

My questions have evolved over the years, and I look forward to their continued evolution. I started with seven questions; now there are twenty.

If they help you, terrific. If they don't, please disregard them. Just understand that you must come up with your own approach. Find your way to the work however you can. The goal is to never get caught acting. The goal is to become that character in every cell of your body because, when you go in front of the camera, everyone else better damn well believe you're that character, too.

Twenty Questions

If I gave you all the questions to an exam, how would you do? And if you'd already worked out the answers before you sat down, then how would you do? You couldn't fail to ace the exam if you knew all the questions and all the answers.

The goal of these twenty questions is freedom. They're a way of making sure you're prepared, giving you the freedom to go into the casting session or on set knowing you've done your homework. Preparation creates confidence, and that confidence is absolute gold.

Some of these questions may seem rudimentary—basic stuff from Acting 101. Some may seem more important than others. But over the years, my clients' results have demonstrated their fundamental value.

1. What Is the Genre?

It seems the most obvious question in the world—"Well, of course, it's a comedy!"

OK, it's a comedy. But is it more like *Animal House* or *Being There*? *Groundhog Day* or *Bridesmaids*?

What type of comedy is it? What are those comedy rules? What is the tone? And, finally (and most difficult to answer), is there a new tone in here, a twist—is this an original comedy voice?

In the theater, it's fairly easy to identify different genres of plays. But in film, and particularly television, the definition isn't always easy. Especially in network television's "pilot" season, many new tones are experimented with— everybody's trying to create a "brand new" television experience.

In the 1980s, *Hill Street Blues* was a new kind of police procedural, with multiple story lines. Before *The Office* in the early 2000s, we'd not seen the "mockumentary" style of comedy on television, with the characters followed around by a documentary film crew. (I believe Rob Reiner's brilliant 1984 movie *This Is Spinal Tap* was the first feature film to rely on this type of comedy.) Today that conceit is old hat; in its infancy, it was difficult to identify.

Genre identification in acting has parallels in dance. You may be a good dancer, but if you think the song is hip-hop and it's actually a modernized waltz, you're going to be off rhythm. That doesn't mean you're a bad dancer; it simply means you didn't identify the genre properly and fell into the wrong rhythm.

A few years ago, one of my clients was hired for an eight-episode arc on a popular television show. On his second day of shooting, I received a panicked text from him.

"Craig! They're going to fire me."

This is an actor who should not be fired from anything, because he's really good.

I jumped in my car, ran over to the Warner Brothers lot, and went to his trailer.

"Let's read," I said. "Show me what you're doing."

He read as if it were a drama, like it was the most serious piece of *Law and Order*, or a somber Spike Lee movie. He was so serious!

"What planet is this?" I asked. "What genre?"

He looked at me anxiously. "Comedy?"

"Close! It's a dramedy. It's fun for the most part, but once every scene they get serious. You need to have more fun."

He was playing a political character. I said, "Imagine you're Bill Clinton, and have fun with it." He read it once and killed it. I was in the trailer for all of fifteen minutes. They didn't fire him.

Driving home, I realized this question underpins everything from the start. It's the first question to ask. If such a fine, experienced actor could make such a basic mistake, anyone could.

2. What Are the Traps?

A trap is anything that will get you caught "acting."

The first trap can often be found in question 1. The genre itself can be a trap. Doing the genre is a trap. The drama trap is being overly dramatic. Shakespeare is a huge trap. Well, it's Shakespeare! Shouldn't you be spewing some stagey, formal, quasi-British nonsense?

Trying to be funny is a trap. Lots of films are funny because the actors are completely committed to the truth of the script. Think of Robert Downey Jr. in Ben Stiller's 2008 film *Tropic Thunder*. Or Madeline Kahn in the 1974 Mel Brooks classic *Young Frankenstein*.

One of the things that makes these performances so funny is that the actors are not trying to be funny. They're not trying to schedule a laugh. If the funny bit doesn't land where they expected, if the chuckle happens to end up with the other actor, so be it. They don't chase funny; they let funny happen.

Another trap is the writer's parentheticals ("she cries," "he screams," "with great intensity," etc.). The worst thing you can do is fall directly into these traps. Why? Because appointments are the death of acting.

If you take on the appointment a writer has given you in the script, you're in danger of getting caught acting. Crying on cue doesn't make you a good actor. If the emotion is forced or purely technical, the audience will know and won't trust you. Your audience at an audition is the casting director and creative team. They'll know quickly whether you're "acting" or living truthfully under the imaginary circumstances.

Rather, look at the writer's parenthetical as a guide to the stakes in the scene. The writer is indicating the stakes for the character. It is then your job to go deep inside the script and answer the questions about the character's inner life that will guide you to being in the zone of those stakes at that moment.

Do your homework, answer the questions, dig deep inside your personal life, and connect that to the character. Give the character a true and vulnerable emotional reality, then live in the moment. If you happen to cry or scream or experience any other emotional reality, so be it. If the emotional value is different from what the writer has written in the parenthesis, that's OK. Often, a good actor will surprise a director, writer, producer, and even themselves when their emotional heart is open to the event.

"Green" or inexperienced actors often believe it's their job to hit the exact moments as written in the script. This is a mistake. It's your job to take on the circumstantial truth and live fully committed to your emotional center, stay connected to your fellow actor, and let the truth be the truth.

Blanket appointments of "I have to be good," "I have to be funny," or "I have to be sexy" will mess you up as badly as the above appointments. I call these blanket appointments "tone bubbles," because they trap you into a singular tone of voice and create one-note performances. Avoid these at all costs.

Accents can be traps. When an actor falls into stereotypes and over-does an accent almost to the point of parody, the audience squirms at such actorbation.

The worst trap of all is to stay in your head and not go through your gut. Because we value being smart and right, and we so badly want to get the part being smart and right, an actor often gets an answer to a question that is smart and excites them, because they know they've found a great connection to the character.

Staying in your brain, however, and acting the "idea" from there, is prob-ably the number one trap for all actors. It is so enticing to show how smart we are! The head isn't just a trap; it's the enemy.

Most flawed performances happen when an actor falls into a trap and gets caught lying. I could list many bad performances, and I don't mean to be harsh or judgmental, but most actors who give us flawed performances simply aren't aware of the traps they're falling into.

3. What Are the Circumstances?

This is basic script analysis. It's knowing the general breakdown of the action of the scene. That means understanding who the characters are, the arc of the scene, and what's happening.

A scene can trap an actor. From the moment you receive it, you focus on your character alone; the trap is to be drawn slowly into a myopic state of self/character awareness. You're stuck in quicksand.

A good idea is to state aloud, as if you were a viewer of the scene, exactly what's going on. Who are the characters and what's the event? This helps you stay aware of what your actual job is, where your character fits into the bigger picture, and how you can best be of service to the creative team.

In short, make sure you know what's going on! Make sure you understand the big picture as well as the smallest details. That includes any scientific, medical, legal, or police jargon, or any other verbiage with which you're unfamiliar. Make sure you understand it.

A great question is, "What's my status?" Often, young actors want to play the dominant status, but there is terrific wealth in finding the fun of playing subordinate characters as well. (Sadly, most female actors know this all too well.)

And remember, a character's status changes from scene to scene. An example: You're playing the parent of a young child who has misbehaved in class. You're called to the principal's office. In your scene with the female principal, she has the higher status and you, as the "bad" parent, have the lower. In the next scene, where you're driving your child home, you have the higher status.

Breaking down a scene includes knowing its arc. It also means knowing its individual beats. What's a beat? Human beings speak in natural rhythms. Question and answer. Statement and rebuttal. Good writers write in these natural rhythms. Good actors identify these rhythms and play within them.

You should be as knowledgeable about the whole scene—not just your character's place in it—as the writer and creative team. When you go in the audition room, you need to be as knowledgeable as anyone there. If you have a fundamental question, ask it. (But only if it's truly fundamental. Don't waste the creative team's time and energy with baloney, trivial questions.)

You'd be hard pressed to find a more intricate tale than Charlie Kaufman's screenplay *The Eternal Sunshine of the Spotless Mind*. The actors had a big assignment to prepare for and navigate the many levels of an intricate plot. Remember, too, that most scenes in a film are shot out of order, so you need to be aware of exactly where you are in the script—what has already transpired and what's yet to happen. Watch Kate Winslet and Mark Ruffalo. They're especially good.

4. Who Am I?

This is the opportunity to dive deeply into who your character truly is. Do a basic Psych 101 evaluation of their life. What's their psychological makeup? Their race, religion, education, financial history, spirituality, and sexuality? Where were they born, what's the family history, what psychological issues are they dealing with—depression, addiction, abuse? Ask other revealing questions as well, such as, "What does love mean to this character?"

Remember that one of the most impactful determinants of anyone's character is the change they've gone through. A simple example is finances. If a character was born poor and is now wealthy, that's a major change. What if the character's gone from rich to dirt poor? How would that affect them?

"Who am I?" is a wonderful opportunity to find out the fundamental differences between you and the character, as well as the fundamental similarities. You'll see how you can use yourself to be this person, but also where you can't use your own experience because it's so different from the character's.

Character psychology is a gold mine. Why is my character motivated to take this action or make that cutting remark? What is the deep psychology behind it? Answering these questions can only make you better, because they help you find the motivations for your character's actions in their deep psychological background.

Make a list of the answers to these basic questions on the left side of a blank page. On the right side, identify the ways in which you're different from the character. Where you're similar, it's fairly easy to meld your own traits with the character's. Where you're different, however, you must find your personal connection to the character's personality trait.

For example, the character you're playing is a murderer. You (I hope) are not. Somehow you must find a connection to the capacity of taking a human life. Think of the many mosquitoes you've killed. Ants, wasps, and mice? Did you ever have to put an animal down? Now it's just a matter of replacing living creatures with human souls. Your character sees human beings the way you perhaps see mosquitoes: irritating, worthless, disposable.

At the start of your career, you're likely going to be cast for your essence. Even though you're unlikely to get huge character roles, that doesn't mean you shouldn't know how to be prepared, connect your honest emotions to the character, and live truthfully. We'll address deeper character work in more detail in question 14.

There are actors who essentially bring themselves to every role they play. Think of Michael Caine or Reese Witherspoon. They are delightful actors, and most of their performances are based on a soulful connection. They connect to the character's truth and work from there.

5. What Is the Motivation?

Motivation is key to all human behavior. Why do we do what we do? These five motivation questions will help connect you deeply to your character's behavior.

5A. WHAT IS MY OBJECTIVE?

The objective (or "super objective") is the overall goal the character wants to achieve in the scene. This is generally easy to identify and easy to answer with information you've gained from question number 3, "What are the circumstances?"

There are times when a character can have the same objective for many scenes in a row. For example, the characters in *Titanic* have a single major objective for the entire second half of the film—to survive.

5B. WHAT AM I DOING? (WHAT IS MY ACTION?)*

The action is what the character does to achieve their objective. The action is also known as the "doing." If you don't know what you're doing, you're not doing anything. We're not talking about physical actions here; we're talking about the emotional motivation.

The root of the word action is "act"! To take action is to act. You're an actor. You do things. The director doesn't call "Thought" or "Emotion." The director calls "Action!"

"What am I doing?" is the most important question to ask about every scene. If you haven't answered it deeply and personally, and connected it to your vulnerable truth, then you won't be doing anything. You must know what you're doing and what is making you do what you do.

This can be a difficult question to answer. Due to the overwhelming number of details you're processing as you break down a scene and memorize the lines, it can turn into what I call "actor math." But it's vital that you answer the question. And don't just take the easy way out; go deep.

Because answering this question can get heady, I suggest you put pen to paper and write down all the possible actions in the scene. Slowly weed out the less powerful actions until you find the deepest and most powerful. You may also find that you can combine several different actions into one main one.

Back to *Romeo and Juliet*. In the balcony scene, they're essentially doing the same thing. They're both breaking away from their families. They're going against society. They're going against the church. They're undergoing a sexual awakening. They're both looking to the cosmos for a sign that they aren't going mad. If you boil all those things down into one doable action, you might say that they're stepping into their adult selves for the first time. They're stepping into their personal power, taking control of their lives, and becoming their own people.

Another example. You're playing a male character on the phone with your girlfriend. You're apologizing for having slept with her best friend the night before. Ask yourself: What am I doing? What is my action?

You could say that you're talking on the phone. That's an action. You could also say that you're apologizing. That's an action. You could say that you're saving the relationship—also an action, and one that goes deeper than mere apology. You could say that you're saving your life, because you cannot live without her. Now, that's an action!

All those actions are valid interpretations, but which one is the deepest? The last one, obviously. And usually, the actor who goes deepest wins the role.

When you're working out the action/doing, remember that 80 percent of all human action grows out of three things: love, fear (or the need to survive), or the desire for material gain. So right away you can go to those motivations and see how they connect with the character's behavior. That can be an easy way to access the deeper answers.

Making a deep, visceral connection to your action can make the work almost easy. The action, when it's deeply realized, is like a magic carpet that flies out in front of you for the scene. You're safe to go anywhere because you know it will catch you. You can run around, do backflips, take a long pause, or fly like crazy, because that carpet stays under you, always there to catch you.

Be careful, though, that the doing doesn't overwhelm every beat of the scene. In the Stanislavski Method, you can put a different action on almost every line of dialogue if you wish. I don't coach this approach; it feels too controlling. You want to have some room to play. And if you have a very strong overall action, the smaller actions are simply fun discoveries in playing the scene. The action shouldn't throw you off the plot line the writer has created. It simply gives you motivation. It gives you something to do.

Make certain that you make a choice. Do something. Most directors and casting directors don't care if you're wrong; if you are, they'll tell you. But what they don't like is an actor who doesn't make a choice—doesn't do something. (Some people call an "action" an "intention." That has always seemed a funny word to me because it can convey intent without action. But if "intention" works for you, terrific.)

5C. What Do I Want?
The "want" is the dream scenario for the character. The best possible outcome of the scene. For our character on the phone, his "want" might be for his girlfriend to forgive him, allow him to return to the way things were, and pretend his infidelity never happened.

5D. What Do I Need?
The "need" is the bare minimum for the character. For our character above, his "need" might be for some sign, any sign, that his girlfriend might possibly forgive him. A light breath, a little laugh, an inflection—any sign that he might be able to salvage the relationship.

5E. What Am I Looking for in the Other Actor's Eyes?*
In life, we don't watch ourselves. We look into the eyes of the people we're engaged with. Why, then, do actors watch themselves when they're working? You should be seeking something from the other character's eyes. And if

you never get from them what you're looking for, that's a good thing! Keep seeking.

This can be very helpful when you have a bad reader in an audition. If you are looking for something in their eyes that they never give to you, that is great. That means you have to stay focused and intent on receiving the results you desire.

THE TWO CRUCIAL QUESTIONS

Note the asterisks on questions 5B and 5E. These are the two questions you must answer fully. I tell my clients to never be at an audition or on set without having answered those two questions and deeply connected the answers to your gut. This is fundamental. It is crucial. Most bad acting comes from actors who haven't answered those two questions.

In life, when two people are talking, two key things are going on. Both people are doing something, and both need to see something in the other person's eyes. This is particularly true when there's a lot at stake. Every good writer creates stakes for all of the characters.

Let's take our cheating boyfriend off the phone and put him face to face with his girlfriend. The boyfriend has an action—seducing the girlfriend into believing his lie that he didn't sleep with her best friend. What he needs to see in her eyes is that she believes him. For her, the action is to deduce whether he's telling the truth. What she needs to see in his eyes is honesty.

This creates an energy loop between both characters that flows continuously from the action and the need in their eyes. In life, this is the energy that infuses a conversation with something at stake. Now, of course, both people have their history—who they are, where they come from, and all of the life information inside them—but they're not talking about those things in that moment. They're focused on the action and what they need to see in the other person's eyes.

That energy is what you want to create when you work with a fellow actor. And that energy, that give and take, that energy loop cycle of action and need—it's palpable. It's what the camera picks up. The camera captures that energy, and if it's truthfully grounded, coming from the actor's gut and soul, the audience will see it as well. As Michael Douglas said, "The camera can tell when you're lying."

I suggest to my clients that the last thing they do before the camera rolls, on set or in an audition, is to ask those two crucial questions: "What am I doing?" and "What do I need from the other character's eyes?" Hold onto the answers. And then, when they call action, your action and your need will roll out in front of you, a magic carpet, and off you go.

Those questions are also the secret to doing a good cold reading. No one in a casting office or at a cold reading expects an actor to be able to memorize an entire scene in five minutes. To waste time on memorization is a big mistake. Instead, focus your attention on the two questions, answer them, connect the answers to your gut, and work directly from the script while connecting with your reader. Chances are you'll deliver.

6. Why?

Now, we immediately ask "why" about the previous motivating questions. Why is this my objective? Why am I doing this? Why do I want this? Why do I need this? Why am I looking into their eyes for this? And the answer should be something like "or else I will die."

The "why" makes you go deeper. It builds upon the motivation question. Again, I believe those who go deepest usually win.

For example, our cheater on the phone with his girlfriend has a strong "why" that goes through all of the motivational questions. Why does he need her forgiveness? Because he will fucking die without her.

7. What Are the Relationships?

Who are the others in the scene, and what do they mean to you? Ask yourself what every other character means to your character. What is the essence of the relationship? Once you understand that, you can delve into your own life and find people who approximate those relationships. If there's no match in your life, use your imagination.

An example: A courtroom scene between a judge and a lawyer. Some actors might say respectfully, "Your Honor," and the audience will view it as a basic social interaction between judge and lawyer. But what if that judge is a wonderful citizen, an honorable man who holds to the letter of the law, who is not a racist or sexist, who is fair and kind and wise?

Well, if I were playing the lawyer, I'd substitute my respect for my father for my attitude to the judge, because those qualities describe my dad. If the judge were corrupt and venal and unjust, I'd substitute my relationship with my ex-friend Billy. And you'd hear the difference when I said "Your Honor" to a man with Bill's dubious moral character.

Another example. You're in a dining scene. You could view the busboy at the restaurant simply as a servant, or you could treat him with sympathy, or derision, or as a potential sexual hookup. The fun is up to you—just don't distract from the script and the story being told.

8. What Is My Obstacle and How Do I Get Around It?

A good writer will create an obstacle for every major character in almost every scene. The character will take an action to get over that obstacle, which may or may not succeed. The action is our concern here, because what people do—the choices they make when there's something at stake—reveal character. The choice of action reveals a character's moral code.

For example, a police officer finds illegal contraband in your character's car. How your character reacts is very telling. One type of person will lie and deny ownership. A second person will shrug and say, "You got me." There you have their moral code.

One positive way to approach obstacles is to ask: where is the hope in the scene?

9. What Is My Secret?

A wonderful question. What can you privately create that is going on in the character's life that no one else knows about? You do not tell the director, writer, or your fellow actors.

Your secret must always conform to the script, of course, and to the story you're serving. You can't have some wildly crazy secret ("I've got stage four liver cancer!") that has nothing to do with the script. Your secret can't distract from the story's essence.

The point of creating a secret is that it gives you a deeper understanding that the character you're playing is a real person, because we all carry secrets. We all have things going on that we don't reveal. Build your secrets from the places people really do: financial, sexual, personal history, addiction, political, spiritual, and oh so many others!

There's nothing better in a love scene than a secret—a pregnancy, an STD, bisexuality, a secret fantasy. Those are great secrets to have.

Shame is a master emotion to work from here. Secret shame is a great motivator!

Maybe the bride walking down the aisle just found out she's pregnant. If she's another kind of woman, maybe she's pregnant from sleeping with the best man.

Maybe our lawyer is secretly in love with the judge's daughter. Or he happens to know that the judge has serious financial problems.

I once shot a film with Roger Corman. I played the nephew of an emperor. My secret was that I aspired to become the next emperor. It was extremely helpful to me. It meant that every action was intended to help me achieve my goal. It informed the way I treated everyone around me, how I felt about the other characters. It really was a useful secret that carried me through the entire shoot.

Other secrets could be: I'm going to write a book about this. I'm taking notes. Or I'm ashamed of my front teeth, my nose, my ugly ears. Little human things that we all feel from time to time. Truthful insecurities like that help make the character become more real.

One of my clients played a character who was ashamed of his hands through the entire movie. That secret came from something in the script, so he wasn't making it up out of the blue. The writer wrote a line referencing the character's hands, and my actor decided that would cause him to hate his hands. Fun!

Just remember that the secret cannot distract from the scene, and that it can never be told. Only your character knows it. A secret isn't a secret if other people know about it.

10. What Does This Script (Movie, TV Show) Mean to My Life Today?

This question connects directly to your mission as an artist and as a businessperson in this industry. Knowing what a particular project means to you personally is important. You don't have to share this with anyone in the audition room or on set, but you should know for yourself.

It's fine if it's a McDonald's commercial. Sometimes you have to pay the rent. It's OK if it's not the greatest script in the world. Sometimes you work just to work. The dream scenario of picking and choosing the roles you play is rare in this industry. It's OK if the project you're working on is meant to entertain mindlessly—to make people laugh in delight or scream in terror!

The point of this question is to ground you in why, as an actor, you are doing this audition or project. When you walk in the room, the people behind the desk will have already asked themselves that question. And they'll understand implicitly that you have, too. You may not have the same reasons or motivation, but you'll have connected to the script in a personal and business sense as well as an artistic one. And believe me, they're connected to it that way as well.

11. How Do I Make Everything Make Me Better?

As we've discussed previously, a central keystone of my work is to create champions. Champion mindset takes negatives and turns them into positives. We take where we are in our real life and make it work for us.

I'm exhausted. How can I use that?

I'm sweltering. How can I use that?

I'm excited and nervous as hell. How can I use that?

If you make everything make you better, it's really hard to fail. The way to do that is to ask yourself, "How do I feel? Where am I really? How can I make that make the character real?"

You're nervous before an audition. How can your character be nervous? Hamlet could be nervous because he feels that his entire world has been torn down. Juliet could be nervous because she's never slept with a boy. Our lawyer could be nervous because he knows he won't be made a partner of the firm if he loses this case. If you're nervous in front of the casting director, use those nerves to make you real. To make you better.

Think of how professional athletes use pressure to enhance performance. Tiger Woods, on the eighteenth green on Sunday afternoon, putting for a million dollars, is under huge pressure. There's huge money at stake. Add about four hundred photographers, millions of TV viewers, and big money sponsors like Nike and Taylor Made, not to mention Woods's parents, who've done everything in their power to help him to this point.

Instead of letting that pressure make him falter and miss the shot, he uses it to make himself better. That difference in mentality is often the difference between failure and success.

A lead actor on a big-budget film faces the same pressure. If the film bombs and his performance is panned, his career may be in jeopardy. Great actors turn that pressure into a positive motivator. In other words, it's a perspective shift or pivot. Not what are you running away from, but what are you running toward? With diligent practice, you too can learn to transform negative forces into positive inspiration. Doing so will change your career and your life.

12. How Do I Raise the Stakes?

Go back and look at your choices. Go back through all the questions and ask, "Are my stakes high enough? Have I raised the bar? Have I raised the intensity level so that this scene really means something to this character?"

Remember, we raise the stakes with ruthless specificity.

13. What Is My Inner Monologue?

This is a classic, old school Stanislavski question. The inner monologue is what your character is thinking about what the other characters are saying. Write out these thoughts.

For example, our judge, listening neutrally to the lawyer's summation to the jury, might be thinking, "You're missing the mark. Can't you read the jurors' body language?"

Don't memorize these reactions. This is just a way to remind yourself that there's someone else in the scene you should be listening and reacting to.

14. How Do I Explore the Character More Deeply?

This question applies to when you're playing a character completely unlike yourself. We're talking about the kind of complete physical transformation that actors like Daniel Day-Lewis, Tom Hardy, and Hilary Swank are famous for. Here are some ideas to help you explore a character more deeply.

FILTERS

A filter is a point of view or perspective that the character lives with. It colors the way the character sees, experiences, and reacts to the world. Blanche Dubois, a character in Tennessee Williams's *A Streetcar Named Desire*, sees the world through rose-colored glasses. Normal light is too bright for her damaged eyes and brittle soul. The glasses aren't just rose-colored; they're cracked as well. Her view is not clear, the images don't quite line up, and danger is always imminent.

Physical Differences

This is where actors have a great time changing their weight, teeth, hair, eyes, nose, and almost anything else they can change. Picture Robert DeNiro in *Raging Bull*. A great question I've always loved is, "How does the character hold their weight? How do they walk differently from me?"

During reshoots on *Capote* in Harlem, Philip Seymour Hoffman complained to me about his back pain. When I asked what he'd done to hurt himself, he shook his head and replied, "Nothing. Truman just stands differently than me." That's my kind of actor.

Mental and Physical Idiosyncrasies

There is no end to the fun you can have in this zone. Taking your cue from the script and never distracting from the story, you can have a great time creating mental and physical tics. Think of Dustin Hoffman in *Midnight Cowboy* or Jennifer Tilly's wonderful turn in *Bullets Over Broadway*.

Accents

Obviously, accents can make great changes to the characters we play. Just remember to be specific. There's nothing worse than a failed or generic accent; it's one of the worst traps for an actor.

Vocal Placement

Does your character speak in their nose? At the back of their throat? At the tips of their teeth? Or from a squeezed larynx?

COMBINING INFLUENCES

A master of comic character work, Johnny Depp has been known to take different social icons or stereotypes and blend them to create a unique, new, and highly entertaining character. He has said that Captain Jack Sparrow from the *Pirates of the Caribbean* franchise is a blend of Keith Richards, Pepé Le Pew from the Bugs Bunny cartoons, and a hyperactive fourteen-year-old girl.

British film directors Mike Leigh and Francis Lee have both guided their actors to deeply affecting performances using highly specific, in-depth character histories.

When my clients prep for film roles, I structure their homework on the following five focus points.

1. Body and physicality. Find your differences. Be very specific. Generalities will fail you.

2. Script and story. Focus on what the writer gave you to inform your choices. Break down the scenes and answer all the questions. Know the arc of the character's journey in the script. Memorize your lines.

3. Character. Who is this person? Dig deep. Write a character history. Have fun, be inventive, and make the character yours.

4. Spirit and mind. What is at the core of their belief system and moral code? How do they actually think? Begin to think like them.

5. Voice and expression. How do they speak and express themselves? Accent work must be intensely specific and practiced endlessly. I tell my clients to get into the accent and live there. Even at home. Family and friends be damned, you have to be believable.

It is very important to incorporate these areas into believable truths for you. When that camera rolls, you can't be worried about being caught acting. You must simply be.

15. Who Is the Scene About?

The answer to this question should always be the same: Not you! This is a great question to stop you from watching yourself and actorbating. Actorbating is the most boring thing in the world. If you catch yourself, turn your attention to the other actor and look for what you need from them! The scene is always about the other characters. Listen to them. You must know what your character is seeking from the other characters. Look for it, work for it, watch for it, get it!

16. Where Am I?

This is another classic Stanislavski Method question, one that Stella Adler found particularly helpful.

Where you are in the world has an impact on your behavior. Therefore, it's important to know exactly where you are. Sitting in the passenger seat of a meth dealer's old beater in Newark is very different from sitting in the passenger seat of a meth dealer's Range Rover in Santa Monica.

Some actors find it helpful to be specific about where they are before they go into an audition or onto a set. You can create a world around you in your mind. The casting office can be a meadow; the casting director and creative team are a series of hills. Or the room is an art gallery and the casting director and folks behind the desk are all figures in paintings. On a film set, the camera can be a lamp, a statue, or a tree. Use your imagination. Do everything you can to help you believe that you really are that character living under those circumstances.

17. What Is the Sexuality of the Scene?

People are sexual creatures. When you portray a human being, you have to take in their sexuality and understand what drives them sexually. This is not perverted or silly or unethical; it is part of your job. Obviously, you must be professional and not perverted or silly or unethical when you do your work.

Sexuality exists between all characters in a scene, regardless of their relationship or desire. Sexual status in a scene is very real, whether it exists between two straight males, a gay male and straight female, a lesbian couple, or any other combination of the above.

To take this one step further, I believe most truly vulnerable, beautiful performances include an element of sexuality. I don't mean "sexy" or "hot." I mean the deep running river of sexuality that flows through the character. Identify it, then identify with it.

Think of the way these actors have infused their performances with the sexuality of their characters: Julianne Moore, Saoirse Ronan, Sigourney Weaver, Faye Dunaway, and Shirley MacLaine. Male actors who stand out for me include Rami Malek, Mahershala Ali, Brad Pitt, James Dean, and Steve McQueen. One of the things that makes them all wonderful actors is that they bring their characters' sexuality to life in a vibrant, truthfully human way.

Remember, sexuality informs humanity, and humanity is the point.

18. How Am I Vulnerable?

Identify for yourself how the character is vulnerable. You need tremendous confidence to walk into a casting office or onto a set. At times, this confidence can tip an actor away from the lovely qualities that human vulnerability brings to the work. Never forget how beautiful the truly vulnerable are.

A simple question to help you discover this is: What is my character's core damage? What essential damage did they live through that still stays with them and affects their behavior and belief systems?

19. What Is My Moment Before?

This is another classic Method question, and one that I find helpful in setting my clients up for the jump into the scene. What happened, or what was said, just before the first line of the scene? This gives you an immediate kickoff point—it keeps you from getting caught "acting," because you simply continue to live in the moment. When the camera rolls, it just happens to catch you at the first line of the scene.

20. Do I Believe I Am the Character?

Is your bullshit meter going off? If it is, return to the work and find out where you went wrong or where you have not worked deeply enough. Another bullshit alarm? Rinse and repeat until the bullshit meter shuts down.

If your bullshit meter is not going off, if you're confident that you did the work honestly and deeply connected it to your gut, you're ready to go to work. Now give the character your oath of integrity that you will never abandon their truth and you will never get caught "acting."

The Three Oaths

Studying great acting over the years, I'm often struck by the absolute purity— the righteous perfection—of a flawless cinematic performance. Think of Peter O'Toole in *Lawrence of Arabia*. Meryl Streep in *The Iron Lady*. Judi Dench in *Notes on a Scandal*. Joaquin Phoenix in *The Joker*. Frances McDormand in *Fargo*. Ralph Fiennes in *The English Patient*. It's as if these actors have pledged an oath of integrity to the character they're playing—a noble promise, an absolute allegiance to the character's truth.

The oath entails personal humility, a complete lack of ego, and a deep understanding of the terrific energy, focus, and abandonment it takes to create beautiful work. The best actors seem to have a profound respect not just for the character they're portraying, but for the entire history and practice of the work they do.

From my appreciation of what great performances have in common, I've created three brief oaths that I offer to young actors. I do so in the hope that they will develop the same depth of integrity and commitment. Some clients have found the oaths a source of connection, comfort, and inspiration. Perhaps you will, too.

1. The Actor's Oath of Integrity to the Character

I _____, hereby swear my oath to _____ that I will live with complete integrity to your essence. I will bring you to life as an honest function of my spirit/soul, which I will merge with your spirit/soul. I will leave myself at the door and fulfill my obligation to your truth and circumstance without judgment, vanity, or ego. I will not make appointments for your emotions, but rather exist as you and react honestly in your best interests.

2. The Actor's Oath to the Craft

I hereby swear my oath to the art of acting. I vow that I will respectfully treasure the gift of your presence in my life. I commit to the discipline, integrity, craft, and art of being an actor. I will not distract myself with the whims and vicissitudes of ego. I will put craft ahead of material considerations and personal gratification. It is an honor to be an artist. I will protect, uphold, and live up to that honor.

3. The Actor's Oath to Self

I hereby swear my oath to myself. I promise to take care of you spiritually, physically, financially, and emotionally. I vow to hold you accountable. To protect you from danger. To set boundaries on potentially dangerous diversions. To give you peace and rest. To remind you to laugh. I promise, at all times, to elevate you to your highest potential.

Be Specific

Above Sandy Meisner's desk at the Neighborhood Playhouse was a sign that read "Be Specific." I looked at those words often and pretended to comprehend their simple brilliance. In truth, I was confused as to what they actually meant.

I think I now understand. Being specific is essential to achieving quality work. In my experience, you can't be too specific when answering the twenty questions. The more specific my clients are in answering these questions, the more connected and profoundly honest they become.

Don't generalize. Don't grab an easy answer. Specificity, simply put, means "details." The genius really is in the details.

Finally, you must connect the answers to these questions to your belly. It is imperative that you ingest and assimilate the answers into your gut by using a substitution. You then give that feeling in your belly to the character. This final step is often the difference between good actors and great actors.

The goal of all of this work—of answering these questions, digging deep into the script, assimilating those answers and transferring them to the character—is to give you confidence—confidence that you've truly connected to the character from your soul, that you've done your homework, that you're ready to do the work from a fully realized state.

Two actors I greatly admire for their consistent ability to achieve this realized state are Annette Bening and Javier Bardem. They dig deep. They bring their hearts to the work. They make specific and fun character choices. They never take the easy way out. They're committed to bringing the character to life with respect and integrity.

4
Skiing the Scene

Have you ever gone downhill skiing? Or snowboarding? If not, imagine what it would be like to push off and head down a steep, icy slope. From the top of the hill, you look down over the course, gently twisting and turning all the way to the chalet where hot chocolate or mulled wine awaits. Poles in hand, exhilarated, you're ready to go!

Acting a scene is like skiing down a mountain slope you've skied many times before. You can see where you're heading, you know what the terrain's going to be like, you know the conditions, and you know you'll have to do some tight turns through the narrow part of the course. Maybe you're freezing cold, it's the last run of the day, and you can't wait to warm up by the fire.

The thing is, you can't be at the bottom of the hill before you actually get there. You have to safely navigate every mogul and icy patch all the way down. Before you set off, you may do a bit of visualization, but once you start down that slope, the only place you can be is right here, right now. You can't think fifty feet ahead or back to the top of the hill. Your job is to be in the moment. If you get distracted, you're not going to see that mogul until a moment too late.

So, too, with acting. You must stay in the moment with your fellow actor. You must never leave that moment. If you do, you're sure to be distracted and get caught acting. When you've done your homework, you know those moguls are coming and can smoothly work your way right through them.

Think of your two skis as two of the Archibald Questions. Left ski: What is your action in the scene? Right ski: What is your need from the other actor's eyes? These are the guiding principles that carry you safely down the mountain and through the scene.

Think of your ski poles in a similar way. The left one is your in-the-moment muscle. The right is your bullshit meter. These help you stay balanced as you work your way down the course and through the script, ensuring that you never get caught "acting," tumbling toward a broken leg.

I have friends in the industry who executive produce and show run television shows. On occasion, I've been privy to the casting process. My friends have shared the audition tapes of the actors in the running for the roles. It's always interesting to watch the tapes, decide who I would cast, and then see the choices of the network brass.

One characteristic is common among actors who get cast. They don't stay on one emotional note for more than a sentence. They emotionally "ski" the scene—always moving, turning, flexing, leaning. They're never stagnant. They bring different emotions to every line in every take.

Watch Meryl Streep in a scene. On one line of dialogue, she might start off shyly, unsure what she's going to say to her lover; then get brave and say the line with conviction; then be remorseful that she's said it so bluntly and hurt his feelings; then be relieved that she finally gave voice to her frustration.

Humans often have opposing desires at the same time. For example, "You are my best friend and I love you, but right now I want to smack you." To help yourself, ask, "What is my opposing feeling?" This can be a helpful key to finding wonderful room to ski.

You can't plan your precise route down the mountain. Planning means you're making appointments. If you're planning to laugh here or cry there, you're doomed. Why? Because if you're aiming to hit an appointment, you aren't really in the moment with the other actors. If you're making a big run up to some fabulous acting moment, you're making a mistake. Beautiful moments happen when you're truly connected to the script, your character, and the other actor.

You can never do the same run twice. No matter how closely you try to duplicate your last run, it's impossible. Same with a scene in a script. You know the overall arc. You've memorized the lines. You know the beats. You can play all the way through the scene, truthfully in the moment with your fellow actor. You can speed up. Slow down. Change the emotional tone from line to line.

Don't ever let yourself get locked in, trying to repeat what you just did. If you do, you're no longer truthfully in the moment. You can change your speed and direction, but those changes need to come organically, never from an idea of what the scene is "supposed" to be. It's your run; have fun!

And what would be the fun in doing a scene exactly the same way twice? Why would you make an emotional appointment? Remember, appointments are the death of acting. If you've done your homework, answered the questions, assimilated the answers, and are living truthfully as the character, go for it and let the scene unfold in a way that's as exciting, dangerous, and exhilarating as a black diamond run.

Have you seen Marlon Brando in Elia Kazan's film of Tennessee Williams's *A Streetcar Named Desire*? Brando is considered one of the great actors in film history, in part due to his amazingly truthful and volatile performance as Stanley Kowalski. By the time they made the movie, Brando had performed the role on Broadway more than eight hundred times. How did he keep his performance so fresh and alive and unplanned? He skied!

More recent daredevil skiing can be seen in Timothée Chalamet's portrayal of Elio in Luca Guadagnino's film *Call Me by Your Name*. There's no sense of self-awareness in his work. He has a lovely freedom in front of the camera. As with Brando, you never quite know what he's going to do next.

That's because he doesn't, either.

Part II
THE DISCIPLINE

5
Tools

Ah, discipline, that bitch of a word. A word to both hate and love in a single breath! Whenever I hear it, my brain switches off. I feel annoyed or in need of a nap. Well, naps can be wonderful and empowering, but they can also be a sign of laziness and depression.

Merriam Webster defines *discipline* as "training that corrects, molds, or perfects mental faculties." I like that description. It brings us to the next step in your life as an artist, beyond Method and training. It speaks to a deeper commitment, the ability to self-command and achieve mastery. Mastery is the goal. To achieve it, you need to know and perfect the tools of your trade.

If you were a young baseball player aspiring to a professional career, you'd strive to master a particular set of skills. Derek Jeter mastered all the primary baseball skills: hit for average, hit for power, run, field, throw. If you were a nine out of ten in all of those skills, you'd have a shot at becoming a professional. If you were a seven or eight, your chances would be slim to none.

The same is true as you strive to become a professional actor. There are specific skills you need to master. At the Archibald Studio, we begin by assessing each of your acting tools. That shows us what you need to work on to improve your technique, craft, and method.

You need a polished skill set before you start auditioning. Casting directors can be forgiving of young actors, but they won't excuse amateurism indefinitely. The higher your skill level, the more likely you are to get a callback. The more callbacks you get, the more likely you'll book a job.

For many, acting feels unquantifiable. These tools are the remedy to that feeling.

The Ten Tools

1. Breaking Down a Script

This is simple script analysis 101. You break down the beats of the scene, identify all the story points, spot any problem areas or traps, and clarify the circumstances. You identify any obvious laugh lines and define any medical, political, criminal, or legal jargon. You dissect the scene looking for obstacles, objectives, and motivating factors for every character.

Who are these people? What's going on here? What's the event? What are the circumstances? What's happening in this scene? Who is my character? Where do I fit into the story? Am I a lead or supporting character? Who are all the other characters and how do I relate to them? What literary devices has the writer used (flashbacks, voiceover, dream sequences, etc.)?

You investigate every detail so that all the decisions we make in creating your character are based in the truth of the written script. Good writers create an obstacle and a resolution in every scene. You must identify these.

According to the Method, remember, you must ingest the answers to all of these questions using substitutions that pinch you into a true emotional connection to the circumstances of the scene. This may sound easy, but it takes time. The more you do it, the better you'll become. This is especially important during a busy pilot season, when you may get more than one audition a day. Breaking down scenes is critical to your success.

Should you not understand some aspect of the scene, it's imperative that you clarify that with the casting directors before you audition. Believe me, they won't mind. They want you to be good.

Several years ago, at the end of an exhausting pilot season, I was coaching my final class of the week before taking a ten-day break. One of my clients had an audition the next day. As he prepped his dramatic scene with me, I heard whispering and giggles from the rest of the class. I finally turned and said, "Um, excuse me?" They thought the scene wasn't a drama. They all thought it was a comedy.

Normally I'm confident in my perspective, but I was so tired I gave in to their persuasive argument. The actor in the chair tried it as a comedy, changed the tempo, and landed a few jokes. I put it up to exhaustion that I had misread the scene.

The next day, my client went into the audition. After doing a brilliantly funny comedy turn, complete with a "button" at the end, he was asked by an insulted writer, "What made you think this was funny? It's a dramatic scene."

Break down the script properly. And if you have any doubts? Ask!

2. Sense Memory

We experience life through our senses. We hear, see, taste, smell, and touch. If that's how we humans experience life, that's how the characters we play need to experience life as well.

The memory of your senses is a crucial mechanism for your work. You use it in your substitutions (in both memory and imagination) and in developing the imaginary circumstances under which your character lives.

Let's return to *Romeo and Juliet* in the balcony scene. You're ingesting the answer to the question "What are you doing in this scene?" down into the gut, using a substitution. The answer, remember, is: "I'm seizing my power and becoming my own person for the first time in my life."

I'll cast myself as Romeo and recall a moment when I seized my power and became my own person by moving to London. I can see the Saskatoon airport, the groovy overhead lighting from the 1980s, the polished redbrick walls, and my family gathered to say goodbye as I'm about to leave them behind. I can see the navy blue travel jacket my brother handed me as a parting gift and the excitement and pride in his eyes. I can smell the reek of jet-fuel exhaust that permeated the airport and my father's deodorant as he leaned in to kiss me. I feel his tears on my cheek. I hear his shaky voice. My vision is blurry through my tears.

As I turn away and leave them and move toward security, I feel a roaring engine in my chest. This is what it feels like to seize my power. At this point, the memory is in full Technicolor, and I'm having a visceral emotional reaction. I'll bring this sensation to my character, Romeo, as I approach Juliet's balcony.

Now you be Romeo. Use your sense memory to develop the reality surrounding your character in the actual scene—not from memory now, but from imagination. Revisit your senses in the garden in Juliet's yard.

What can you visualize about the space you're in? What's the lighting? How bright is that moon? Can you see it glistening on the water in the fountain? Can you differentiate the foliage in the garden? What are the shadows of the surrounding buildings?

What are the smells in the garden? Is there night-blooming jasmine? Can you smell the cold, damp earth? Is there a breeze filled with the honey of an Italian spring evening?

What can you taste? Perhaps the paste you used to clean your teeth, or the mint you've chewed to freshen your breath?

What can you hear? Crickets? Frogs? The water in the fountain gurgling? And how about far-off noises from the street, perhaps horse hooves on cobblestones? What about voices? Can you hear what your parents would say if they saw you right now? Can you hear what your inner voice is saying?

And finally, what do you feel? The chill of the night air? Your heart pounding in your chest? The powerful soul-consciousness of becoming your own person?

By examining those different sense memories and focusing from one sense to the other, you can create a reality for yourself and bring it all to life.

Sense memory is a beautiful gift to your life as an actor. It can actually change the way you live, because you become a connoisseur of life. It can change the way you experience the weather, the moment, and the life that you're living. Right now, take in the quality of the light as you read this, the sounds you can hear, the beautiful lilac by the back door. Can you smell it?

The more you learn to use your sense memory, the richer your life will be and the richer your work.

3. Imagination

Your imagination is the playground of your work. When you combine it with sense memory, it can be an outstanding tool to plow the fertile fields of your life experiences, to stimulate and create vibrant imaginary events that emotionally connect you to the character's reality.

Take someone you love and imagine them in a hospital bed. Now visit your sense memory of a hospital. Picture your loved one with eyes closed, face bruised, and tubes in their nostrils and down their throat. Hear the sounds of the monitors and machinery used to keep them alive. Focus on the disturbing sounds of others being ill, calling for nurses, the constant activity of people moving up and down the hallway. Smell the horrible smells: vomit, urine, medicine, disinfectant, sad food. Visit the feelings the room gives you—sadness, worry, fear that your loved one may not survive. Let those feelings settle deep inside you.

That exercise should have an emotional effect on you. If it doesn't, work harder at it. Go deeper.

Now use your imagination in a happier way. You're about to walk onto a soundstage where you'll be working with Wes Anderson and Bill Murray! It's a dream-come-true moment. Go through the same detailed sensory exercise. Smell the stale air in the cavernous space. Notice the way the lights shine on the set. What sounds can you hear as the crew settles into a rehearsal? How does all this sensory input make you feel? Happy and proud and fully alive?

Your imagination is a hugely important tool, one you must become expert at using. Always take time to imagine different scenarios in your busy life. Use your imagination and your sense memory to inhabit difficult moments and wonderful ones. If you can't imagine, richly and specifically, you won't become much of an actor.

4. Emotional Preparation

Emotions—your ability to access them and your capacity to do emotional preparation—are central to your success. Your emotional life is the reservoir you visit to retrieve the essential elements of your work.

As mentioned in the Method chapter, your emotional quotient is vital. This is part of what makes actors different from "civilians." To do your job properly, you have to be sensitive. This can be both healthy and unhealthy, a blessing and a curse. It's important to know when and how to use your sensitivity for the good of your work, and not to the detriment of your lives and loved ones.

If you can tap into your emotional life, be honest with yourself and available to your heart, you can become a good actor. It takes work. It takes attention. It can be especially challenging for young male actors to allow themselves to show deeply vulnerable emotions such as fear and sadness. "Boys don't cry" is a highly damaging dictum. It has far-reaching influence on our society and causes many of my young male clients years of difficulty.

You must prepare yourself emotionally for a scene. Each person is different; no one can tell you how best to connect to your emotions, or which memory or imaginary circumstance will trigger a particular response. This is fun but difficult work for the actor in training. You must know yourself intimately, be aware of yourself, and be able to say, "This is what really makes me angry. This is when I feel compassion. This is how I get when I'm sad. Here's my trigger for happiness. Here's what makes me feel this way."

Acting has a therapeutic quality because it encourages you to go into your life, your memories, and your imagination, then use the emotional elements to bring your characters to life. By doing so, you can actually experience catharsis yourself! Actors use the fears, the horrors, the angers, the frustrations, and, yes, the loves of their lives, to become successful. I think that's a lovely blessing.

5. The In-the-Moment Muscle

This refers to the ability to focus and remain devoutly in the current instant. To disallow your brain to think thoughts outside of your present activity. To be able to fully commit your energy and attention onto your fellow actor and maintain it through any kind of distraction. This is a muscle a young actor must build and maintain. It's the laser-like focus that allows you to jump into the imaginary circumstances with full commitment.

This is a major tool in your work. Here's why: You're living in the moment now. You're in the moment with me, reading this. That feeling, that absorption, is the feeling you want to have when you're acting—the moment-to-moment, living connection with the other actor, going through the moment in an unplanned way. And even though you did the same scene a minute ago in Take One, you're now on Take Two. You must forget Take One and do the scene as if it's the first time you've ever lived it.

You let go of any notion of how things are supposed to go. You let go of any idea of how you did it before, of all the ideas of what worked and what didn't. All outside thoughts are dismissed—thoughts like, "I've got to do it better," or "I've got to be funnier," or "I did this better with Craig in session at the studio and now it has to work here on the soundstage."

You have to be fully, truthfully in the moment with your fellow actor. This is not a trance, or an altered state, but rather a learned ability to sustain concentration through just about anything. You know the way Javier Bardem doesn't even flinch when the car blows up behind him in Ethan and Joel Coen's *No Country for Old Men*, so intent he is on his mission? Like that.

I once watched a major star laugh and joke around between takes on a soundstage and then, when the next setup was ready, snap back instantly and become the sinister creep he was portraying, a character quite unlike the actor himself. That's a highly developed in-the-moment muscle.

The important thing is that you (again, it's on you) must work hard on when your focus is in the moment and when it's not. And here's the crucial element: when you're not in the moment, your trained in-the-moment muscle has to pull you back into focus!

It's OK to have small side thoughts. Normal people have these all the time and, as actors, we are portraying normal people. I call these "brain farts." Green actors think they aren't allowed brain farts and must remain strictly focused at all times. While this state is preferable, don't squeeze for it. Remain in the mental state the character is experiencing. If you have a small brain fart, don't panic or stop the scene. No. These fractious thoughts happen in thousandths of a second, and no one will know unless you tell them. Instead, rely on your well-practiced in-the-moment muscle to bring you back.

Again, this tool is a great gift to your life. Many world religions and spiritual leaders stress the importance of living life in the moment. Your acting training actually enriches your life; it teaches you how to focus and truthfully live in a moment. The most fulfilling life is the one you live when you're fully present.

6. The Bullshit Meter

You use this every day. Your bullshit meter is an innate survival tool. All animals have it; they constantly look out for danger. Your brain has evolved to protect you; that's what it does. It protects you by constantly checking your environment for peril, or threat, or bullshit.

You use it on the street when people approach you. You do a quick check of new surroundings. It's a survival instinct, and it's a valuable tool when you're acting. Your bullshit meter goes off when you realize you're acting, rather than being.

You never want to get caught acting. Ever. Your job as an actor is not to act the part of the character but rather to be that character. Your bullshit meter sits quietly on your shoulder and sometimes whispers, "Bullshit. You're lying. You're acting. Don't do it. Don't push, don't pull, don't pretend. You're not really there. Don't try to cry. Either cry or don't cry, but don't bullshit them. Don't pretend." The bullshit meter says, "Stay here. Be human here, be real."

Your job is to be honest and truthful. Period. Your bullshit meter helps to keep you that way.

7. Memorization

The ability to memorize lines quickly and efficiently is invaluable. I believe that an actor is rarely able to be in the moment if they're trying to remember their lines. So the ability to memorize lines quickly is incredibly helpful.

The first memorization practice I recommend is the penny trick. (You must always do this aloud. In my experience, silent focus on lines rarely produces successful memorization.)

Take ten pennies and place them on one side of the table. Read the first line from the script aloud, then close your eyes and recite the line as written. If you said it correctly, move one of the pennies to the other side of the table.

When you've said the line correctly ten times, move on to the second line. Carry on that way, moving the pennies, until you've said each of your lines perfectly ten times. Then run the entire scene ten times, moving the penny only when you're word-perfect.

Another powerful memorization technique involves recording. Turn on your recorder. First, read all the lines of dialogue—every character's—in order. Don't say the characters' names; just read the scene perfectly off the page, exactly as it's going to sound to the audience.

Don't stop recording. Keep rolling and record the scene a second time, now reading only your lines. Leave yourself enough silent space after each of your lines to repeat those lines when you're in playback—a silent space long enough for you to echo, word for word, the line you just heard.

Leave the recorder running and read the scene a third time. This time, read only the other actors' lines and leave blank space for you to jump in with your lines. When you're in playback for this section, you've left space to say your line on cue and properly.

Now simply loop that one recording, going through the scene repeatedly until your lines become second nature.

These are simple tools that have worked well for my clients. Every actor is different, of course, and you must learn what works best for you. Kevin Horsley's book, *Unlimited Memory*, explains the science of memorization and offers many valuable tips.

8. Memories

Memories are wonderful. They're the library of our lives! They also provide a tool you can use by revisiting as many of your memories as you can. Being specific and using your new knowledge of sense memory can bring memories vividly back into your life.

The goal here is to visit as much of your life as possible—the good, the bad, and the ugly. You need to recall things in such brilliant detail that when you're doing substitution work you can easily access moments in your life that connect you to the emotional state your character's experiencing. Specificity is key.

Here's one of my memories. One hot summer afternoon in 1967, my grandmother Mabel and I were returning to my Uncle John and Aunty Kay's farm after an afternoon of shopping in Birch Hills, Saskatchewan. Grandma stopped the car, a baby blue 1964 Chevy II, at the top of the lane. She got out to retrieve the mail from the mailbox.

There was a slight hill in the front lane of the farm. Unfortunately, my grandmother didn't realize that she hadn't put the emergency brake on. When she got out to get the mail, the car started moving without her.

Slowly, the car began to roll down this little hill with her driver's door still open and me kneeling on the front seat. The lane wasn't steep, but the car could have eventually hit the house or ended up in the small pond we called the dugout.

I was a four-year-old in a moving car. Child seats hadn't even been thought of yet. I remember everything about that moment. I remember the feeling of the car moving quietly forward. I can see the car perfectly. I can smell that old 1964 Chevy. I can see my grandmother through the back window realizing what's going on because I was calling to her, "Grandma!" She turned and started to run. I had never seen my grandmother run as if someone's life depended on it!

As the car drifted toward the dugout, my grandmother jumped in the car and hit the brakes. She braked so hard that I banged my head on the dashboard. She shifted into park, grabbed me, and embraced me, apologizing profusely and crying into my little chest.

Forever on the road.

I felt completely comfortable in my trust that she would save me. I wasn't hurt. I had just enjoyed the ride! I loved seeing her run so hard! I loved her emotion. I loved the adventure. And I loved the smell of her hair products.

That is one of my favorite memories. I can see, smell, hear, and feel every-thing. I can see the sunshine and the dust settling on the car when we stopped rolling. It's a golden, perfect memory. So into my book of memories it goes.

We all have a million memories—trips we took, friends we laughed with, romantic moments, kissing someone lovely. Memories from school. Memo-ries from family. Memories from vacations.

Go on memory trips. Allow yourself to go back and remember things in exquisite detail. While you're there, pay attention to the senses. You'll compile an amazing encyclopedia of extravagant, emotional memories that you can use in your work.

9. Improvisation

Improvisation is the ability to be fully creative and inspired by the moment without a script. There are classic comedy schools that teach improv mostly for the fun of sketch comedy (the Groundlings, Second City, the Upright Citizens Brigade, and many others). I recommend that you take at least a beginner course in improv at one of these institutions. It teaches you to be unafraid to jump in and continue a scene, with or without dialogue.

Every film I've been a part of used improvisation at some point. In serious dramatic television, you're unlikely to use improvisation due to the strict time constraints on most TV sets. Comedy television is another story. There, when time allows, improvisation is common, respected, and appreciated.

The best improvisation comes from deeply connected truth. Knowing who your character is, what they're doing, and what they need gives you the ability to fly freely within the comedy improvisation rule of "yes, and—," meaning you never negate where the other actor takes you, but respond instead with "yes, and—" then carry on with the scene.

10. Identity

When someone speaks of identity as an actor, they're talking about your personal truthful identity. It is absolutely essential that you know and accept yourself—your flaws, your values, and the intricacies of your personal nature. And you must be comfortable with them.

I've found therapy incredibly helpful in my own life and work, and I know many other actors who've benefited from the self-examination good therapists enable. Some people still attach a stigma to the whole notion of therapy, but as an actor you're seeking any tool that can help you understand who you are, so that you can use that understanding in your work.

It is your essence you use to create the characters you play. If you don't know who you are, you'll be creating characters out of an idea and, as we have discussed, that is not what Archibald Studio champion actors do!

So: Who are you? How do you react to things? What do you believe in? What is your spirituality? What is your personal politics? Interrogate yourself. Answer honestly. Be truthful, be brave, and create your work from your essence.

Practice and experiment with the tools the world has to offer you in the exciting adventure of self-discovery. Meditation, exercise, psychotherapy, and community service are but a few examples. Know thyself.

The Tools: Homework

Here are five exercises you can do on your own time that my clients have found especially helpful.

1. Revisit a Memory

Pick a specific memory and revisit it. Use your sense memory and go into the memory and see it, smell it, taste it, hear it, feel it. If it helps, allocate a specific amount of time: fifteen minutes should be enough. Set an alarm and deeply dive into the memory, reproducing all of the thoughts and emotions surrounding the experience. Work on positive memories, work on negative memories—simple life memories that inspire you. Keep a journal or memory book of specific memories and the emotional qualities they trigger.

2. Create an Imaginary Circumstance

Daydream. Go into your imagination and create an event—adopting your dog from the rescue shelter, for example. Now use your sense memories to make that event come to life. Again, see the colors, smell the scents, taste the air, hear the sounds, and feel the details of the event so specifically that it comes to life. You can create positive daydreams, negative daydreams, suspenseful daydreams—all kinds of imaginary circumstances.

I created an imaginary circumstance (my nephew being involved in a snowmobiling accident) that is so vividly alive in my imagination that I've been able to trust it to provoke deeply disturbing emotions, to the point of tears, since the day I created it in 1990.

You want to create a vault of wonderful inspirations for your work. Have different pinches that you've built over the years available to you at all times.

3. The Emotional Workout

This exercise, intended to help young actors get in touch with their emotions, takes half an hour. Set a timer for fifteen minutes. Now select an emotion. I suggest a darker emotion to start with: greed, anger, loss, fear, rage.

Let's use rage. For fifteen minutes, do everything you can to inspire yourself to be filled with that emotion. Use your imagination, use the present day, use your past, use music, use photos—anything to help you get into that emotional state. By the time your alarm goes, you should be in a full-blown rage.

Then, for the next fifteen minutes, move yourself to the opposite, more positive emotion—love, joy, gratitude, celebration, acceptance, generosity. Use everything you can in your arsenal of tools to get to the fullest, most vibrant emotion possible.

It's an exhausting exercise, and you must be careful. Because you're dealing with emotions, you must always remain grounded in reality. Never get completely lost in your imaginary circumstances. It's imperative that you not lose sight of the fact that you're simply doing an emotional exercise.

This is the Ten Percent Rule. Ten percent of you always knows that the gun is fake, that you have to hit your mark for the camera, that the brick wall is Styrofoam. It's a given that you're an actor performing. A basketball player knows without conscious thought that another step and he'd be out of bounds. It's a constant state of low-level awareness.

Again, you should keep a journal. At the end of the second fifteen-minute interval, record the two emotions you worked with and the triggers that made those emotions come to life. If there's a song that inspires you to dance when you hear it, note that. You're going to use it one day. If there's a memory that triggers acute jealousy, make note of it. You're going to use it one day.

4. Create a Character

This can be tremendous fun. Create a brand-new character—someone you and the world have never seen. Create a history. Create a look. Create a voice. An accent. A walk. A mentality. Idiosyncratic characteristics. Dig deep and make the character unique and authentic. Practice being that character in the privacy of your home until you perfect it, then take them out in public and live truthfully as them.

You're not an actor wandering through a shopping mall on a Saturday afternoon. You're a nuclear physicist risking your life to hand over state secrets to a stranger in a shopping mall in return for a suitcase full of cash. Try it. You'll have a blast! (Just don't get arrested.)

5. Watch Movies

If you've not seen the American Film Institute's top one hundred films ever made, you have some movies to watch. And if you haven't seen the best actor and actress Academy Award performances, and best supporting actor and actress, you have even more movies to watch. With more and more streaming services available every day, there's no excuse not to.

6
Mindset

Here's my formula for success as an actor:

Discipline + Time = Integrity

Integrity + Perseverance = Quality

Quality + Opportunity = Success

Give yourself time. It takes time to build an empire. Don't rush into this like a fool. You are an entrepreneur—an entrepreneur in a large business. This business has a lot of layers that it takes time to learn. This business hires quality artists. Don't think that it can be done overnight. Every "overnight success" you hear of has actually been in the works for years.

The fastest I've taken a client from beginner to working actor is three years. My experience with movies is that they take, on average, six years from conception to completion. A friend of mine adapted his book as a feature film. From the first draft of his screenplay to the first screening of the movie: fourteen years.

A young actor who doesn't understand this process is simply naive. I want you to be smart and savvy. Be disciplined in your practice. Be disciplined at the gym. Be disciplined at class. Do your homework.

The building blocks—the basics of the work we do—always start with the premise that we are physically and vocally trained and ready to perform at any given moment. Too many actors get to Hollywood and give up on their training. Don't do this! Get better and better at your personal discipline. You must warm up physically and vocally DAILY!

Look at it realistically: you're entering a field with many, many competitors. For a call seeking any "type" of actor in Hollywood, there will be at least one thousand applicants for the job. Only the most qualified are going to get a shot. You must be highly qualified. You must be disciplined to achieve your goal. If you've learned discipline, fantastic. I'm proud of you. Now lean into it. Do your time. Take your time. Persevere. Work hard every day, put your head down, and do everything you can to prepare yourself.

When your opportunity arrives, you must be ready. And in my experience, sooner or later everybody gets an opportunity. Be ready for yours.

Discipline over time will make you an artist with integrity. You will know your craft. You'll have your technique. You'll be confident. You'll be smart and savvy. You will not be green and over-eager and seeking validation. You'll be cool and collected, driven by your personal goals. People want to work with people who know what they are doing. No one wants to work with idiots or victims who desperately seek validation or approval.

Gary Oldman is an actor with integrity and commitment to the quality of the craft. He burned bright in his breakthrough performance of Sid Vicious in the 1986 Alex Cox film *Sid and Nancy*, then followed up with twenty years of solid work before finally winning the best actor Oscar, playing Winston Churchill in Joe Wright's *Darkest Hour*. (My favorite is his performance as George Smiley in Tomas Alfredson's 2012 *Tinker Tailor Soldier Spy*.)

I believe that the young British actress Claire Foy may have the same discipline and integrity. She's certainly impressive as Queen Elizabeth II in the Netflix series *The Crown*. I suspect we can look forward to more of that quiet, committed quality.

The Pink Chair

At the Archibald Studio in Los Angeles, the chair where the actors work in front of the camera is a large, soft, and often uncomfortable pink chair. It is initially despised but ultimately beloved by all. It teaches my clients to not be

Class at the Archibald Studio with guest coach Academy Award winner Graham Moore. I'm sitting in the famous pink chair.

precious about their work. It is not the best chair to work in. It is difficult to find a good way to sit. The support is soft. But I purposefully selected it to be the working chair for that reason. Are you really going to say to Mr. Spielberg that you can't act in that chair?

Practice Noise and Distraction

Also, at the Archibald Studio, we do not hold back from chatting and laughing between scenes, particularly while a fellow actor is settling into the Pink Chair. I actually encourage laughter and chatter specifically to challenge my actors to be practiced with noise and distraction. At first people hate this, but it all pays off at the audition or on set where there's no special respect for the concentration it takes to act.

Please Don't Be a Victim

There is nothing more boring in Hollywood than dealing with a victim. Victims are desperate for approval and comfort. There's nothing attractive about being a victim, nothing interesting or funny or inspiring. Never go into an audition or on set being a victim.

That's why I say that I create champions. Champions are attractive. Champions are interesting, funny, and inspiring. A quality artist is a champion. Work diligently, maintain the integrity of your art, and maintain your quality. I promise you will rise.

It is difficult to predict when a quality artist will be recognized. Through my years in this industry, I've seen many people succeed. I've also seen many people put in the time and discipline to become quality artists without achieving great success. All of them have, however, achieved self-worth and self-respect.

Show business is the Wild West. Nobody actually knows how it all works or what's going to be a hit or who's going to make it big as an actor. What we do know is that a life lived as an artist dedicated to the quality and integrity of the art form is a life that will reward you. You will achieve far more than you thought you could, perhaps in ways you never thought you would. You can't do it for the spoils. There's tremendous value in a life lived in the pursuit of artistic excellence. The journey is the goal.

This is what your parents, family members, and civilian friends may not understand. They won't understand why you're living the way you are. They care about you and are concerned for your well-being—and you should love them for that—but they may not understand life as an artist.

You are not a civilian. You may sacrifice a great deal to be able to do what you do. To friends and family, it may sometimes seem like insanity. They don't understand the reward we get when we do our work, and we do our work well, and it is received and celebrated by our fellow artists who understand the discipline, integrity, and quality it takes to achieve the highest level of art.

What your family and friends hopefully will respect is your commitment to the profession of acting. That will make sense to their civilian souls. When you become a businessperson with goals and advisers and a team of professionals who are all focused on achieving the same goal, your life will make sense to your family and friends, and they will give you rock-solid support.

What civilians don't understand is a foolhardy naïf with no business or art sense, someone who's attempting to be a "star" in order to achieve celebrity and red-carpet nonsense. That's also what producers, directors, agents, managers, and casting directors (and this particular acting coach) cannot bear either.

Turn Discipline into Freedom

There are times that discipline can feel like a burden. It can feel "un-fun." It can feel like you are being controlled. The challenge is to turn discipline into freedom. If you can do that, you'll have a different kind of power. You can be in absolute possession of your will.

You have the freedom to choose whether you want to be disciplined or not. If you choose to live with discipline, you'll soon learn that it creates positive habits. Positive habits create positive results. And positive results give you freedom.

If freedom is the goal, and the route to freedom is discipline, then discipline is the freedom to do what you want to do.

Confidence

I can't overemphasize the importance of confidence in this industry. Not cockiness. I'm not talking about walking into the room, taking control, and proving to everyone that you're a great actor. When you do that, all you're doing is showing them that you're trying to prove to them you're a good actor without actually doing good work. That's "green," as I'll explain below.

Chutzpah alone can often be the difference between success and failure. Again, I am not talking about exaggerated bravado. I am talking about deeply focused and powerful confidence. The kind that is only created out of hard work, discipline, and focus.

A confident performer walks in the room, confident in their choices, supported by the knowledge that they've done the work, know the character, and can bring the truthful essence of that character to life. Simple. Deeply researched. Specific. Honestly connected. That's confidence.

I learned this lesson from casting director Vince Liebhart. Vince was the casting director of *As the World Turns* back in the mid-1990s. He called me in for a small role in my early career. When I sat in his office, I suddenly got a bad case of nerves. My breathing got tense and my hands started to shake. Vince looked up from his desk and noticed my condition. He smiled and said, "Don't worry, Craig. You're a good actor."

Thanks, Vince. It just felt so good to hear that! That's all I needed. My confidence returned. I relaxed, focused, committed, and booked the role.

Being Green

"Green" describes newcomers to the business. It's generally used to characterize young actors who haven't trained to the point of professionalism or stage actors who haven't learned the secrets of good camera acting.

It's also used when an actor doesn't understand the politics of the work or is immature in their professionalism. Many young actors have a silly misunderstanding of the work and what the job is all about. It's not about how big your trailer is. It's not about being a star. It's about the work. The craft. The art.

Tantrums

Professional businesspeople generally don't cry at the office. Don't throw a tantrum or sulk on set. Professional decorum is important whether you work at the White House or on the Warner Brothers backlot.

Be a pro. Make everything make you better. If you have to cry or throw a tantrum, do it at home. Actors who have meltdowns on set quickly develop a reputation, no matter how beautiful or gifted they may be. You want to be known as a dependable, respected, collaborative professional.

Don't Get Too in Your Head

It's easy to think too much. Your goal is to be technically precise and yet emotionally spontaneous. All the lessons you learn, all the advice you get, all the information you absorb, you must put to use in service of the work. An oven turns a dozen ingredients, stirred together in a mixing bowl, into a delicious cake. The heat of performance turns all that you've learned into a living, breathing, fully realized character.

Vulnerability

Always work from a place of vulnerability. Often, the instinct to puff up, peacock, and strut comes from a fear of failure. Breathe. Connect your insecurities and nervousness about the work to the vulnerabilities you've found in your homework about the character, and let them blossom within you, so that the character comes to life in a beautiful, human way.

The secret to beating imperfection is to understand that it is our job to illuminate the human condition. And the human condition is far from perfect! It takes bravery to allow the character you are portraying to use your vulnerable inner self—your perfect and imperfect self. When you are brave and do this in your work, the worst-case scenario is that the outcome may not be what you expected. But you also might be pleasantly surprised! At the very least, you will be in integrity with the character and yourself. Also, you will be authentic.

Remember, the imperfection is not necessarily yours. It is the character's.

Adam Driver's work in *Marriage Story*, Riz Ahmed's work in *The Night Of*, and Laura Linney's work in *Ozark* are beautiful examples of strong, vulnerable performances. All of these gifted artists bring integrity and power to their work while also allowing their personal vulnerability to enrich their humanity.

When Things Go Wrong

Remember your support system. Visit your coach, mentor, advisers, acupuncturist, therapist, masseur, and whoever or whatever helps you survive. Go to the beach or the desert, spend time with nature. Do not get stuck in the mud of confusion and victimization.

FONO

A winning mindset means a certain amount of self-auditing. Do not be afraid to dig deep into your own behavior. Please remember to confront your least attractive qualities with kindness. If and when your brain won't shut off negative opinions, I recommend saying "FONO" loudly to break your negative thought process and ingrained neuropathways. FONO stands for "Fuck Off Negative Opinions."

Mastery of an art form is actually the mastering of our minds. We practice and rehearse under thousands of different permutations of our thoughts and brain activity at any given moment in time, so that when it comes time to perform, we can. We have to be able to drop our own brain activity to assume the brain activity of the character we are playing. This takes tremendous self-exploration and discipline. Once you find your personal process through the quagmire of your mind, you are on your way to mastery. Part of that mastery is knowing when your negative thoughts are not helping.

Drugs and Partying

Don't overdo it. If you want a career in Hollywood as an actor, it's like trying to win a gold medal at the Olympics. You absolutely must be world-class. You have to understand that drugs and alcohol, though they may seem "fun" and "cool," will work against your goals.

I'm not saying that you can't have the occasional beer or smoke. What I am saying is that the image of the Hollywood party scene as cool and druggy is real; it does exist. But the people at those bars and parties are not the ones who are on film and television sets the next morning. (And if there is a celebrity at a party who is on set the next day, they're not at the top of their game. They're probably on their way out.) This industry is intensely competitive, so you have to be at your best!

If you do drugs or drink heavily every day, you won't be a successful actor for one simple reason: Drugs and alcohol numb your emotions. Emotions are the raw materials from which you create your value. Create a product or service from inferior materials and you'll have an inferior product or service.

My own life has been deeply damaged and scarred by the effects of drugs and alcohol. When I was a young actor, I would never have guessed how many friends and family members I would lose to the excesses of partying. You only have one brain. It's a delicate and complex organ we don't fully understand.

When you mess with your brain chemistry, you're messing with your life. Please take this preachy sermon to heart. I don't want to be one of those boring sober people, but my life has shown me in great detail the tragedy and horror of drug and alcohol abuse. More than one beautifully talented artist I've known has ended up with severe difficulties. More than a handful of wonderful artists I've known have died prematurely because of an overdose, or as a result of depression and addiction.

My acting champions understand when I tell them that addiction gives you short-term pleasure and long-term pain. Discipline gives you short-term pain and long-term pleasure.

My heart breaks when I think of the deaths of people like River Phoenix, Philip Seymour Hoffman, and Heath Ledger. These superb artists all lost their lives to overdoses. Their families lost beautiful, important souls, and we don't get to witness more of their brilliant work. Heartbreaking.

Life Is Like a Sideways Corkscrew

A client was having a difficult start to his career. He's a charming guy with solid acting chops, but he could not get established in the industry. One day, when he was having a particularly bad time, we went to lunch.

He vented until I finally said, "Hey, listen. Life is like a sideways corkscrew. Sometimes you're up and sometimes you're down, but you're always moving forward."

My statement stopped him cold. The change in his expression told me I'd hit a nerve. He sat back, put down his fork, and exhaled. I watched the tension leave his body.

At my next birthday, he invited me out to lunch again and presented me with a self-made gift I treasure. It's a small antique wooden box that contains an antique corkscrew and a silver plate engraved "Always Moving Forward." I'm no Brené Brown, but it helped him see things in perspective. Maybe at the appropriate moment, it will help you, too.

7
Creating Yourself

From 1989 to 1995, my job between acting gigs was at a restaurant in the West Village of Manhattan. It was a charming spot with a wood-burning fireplace, Italian tile, and large copper pans on a white stucco wall. It was called La Focaccia. Though I found it debilitatingly boring to be a waiter, the job supported me and—as luck would have it—introduced me to an incredible array of artists, musicians, journalists, writers, and actors.

One of them was a well-known actor who lived around the corner and often walked his dog past the restaurant. Over time, we became pals. It is abundantly clear now that he is not the finest human on the planet, and we eventually became ex-pals. Whatever his flaws, however, I learned some important lessons from him.

Watching his climb was fascinating. To call him ambitious is an understatement. Whatever it took to succeed, he made it happen. He snuck into parties, opening night celebrations, and casting offices. He demanded action from his agents and managers, and when his tireless networking brought about an audition, he was fully prepared to go in and kill it. He aggressively sought out prey then hunted it down and slaughtered it.

As I watched his career grow, his movie roles increase in size, the creation of his production company, and the awards that accumulated on his mantel, I realized just how much effort it takes to create a thriving business as an actor. It inspired me to take responsibility and actively change my own career trajectory. I'll always be grateful to him for those valuable lessons.

The key lesson I learned watching him work passionately, sometimes viciously, toward achieving his goals in the world of show business was this: you have to do it yourself.

If there's one lesson you take from reading this book, I hope it's that: You have to make it happen. Your career (indeed, your life) is up to you. I made the mistake when I was a young actor—and I find a good 80 percent of the young actors who come into my studio make the same mistake—of thinking that someone or something was going to come along and create my career. This is a profound mistake.

There's something in our upbringing, something in the way we're schooled, something in our respect and perhaps awe of the industry, that makes many people shy about stepping into the industry and declaring, "I am here, I am growing, I am ready to learn and be the best I can be. Trust me, I can do this!"

No One Is Coming to Save You

As kids, we often believe that mom or dad, or a teacher or professor, is going to step in and save us. As young actors, you may think that an agent or manager or casting director is going to step in and save you.

It's highly unlikely. No one is actively looking for the unique qualities you possess—that special joy you're destined to celebrate in your films and television roles. This is a fantasy that will waste your time and slow your progress.

No one is going to show up and do the work for you. You're the only person you can fully rely on. If you can grasp this reality, you'll discover a wonderful freedom, a remarkable power. You really are the master of your life. You are the decider of your fate. The choices you make will define your life. You are completely responsible for the actions you take. This is tremendously exciting!

Your life is in your hands. So reach out and grab it. Take control. Change direction. Make your life what you want it to be. Be smart, get trained, hire savvy advisers, make a game plan, make lists, take action every day, and I promise you—there's a really good chance you'll succeed.

No one can predict exactly when or how you'll succeed. That's part of the fun. In my experience, everyone who deserves an opportunity gets one. Those who are prepared when the opportunity comes are the ones who take the next step. So prepare. Follow your dreams and you'll have a wonderful adventure!

It's not easy. It takes time. It takes discipline. You must learn how to do your best work, what circumstances motivate you, and what choices deplete your energies. You must be driven. You must be practical. You must be wise. And you must do it yourself.

Viva Las Vegas

In 1994, a dear pal, Maggie Moore, sauntered into La Focaccia and told me she had a brilliant idea. She'd spent the summer in Provincetown, Massachusetts, performing her one-woman show *Are You There God? It's Me, Ann Margret*. There, she met a fantastic drag king performer named Julie Wheeler, who did a killer Elvis Presley impression.

Maggie's idea was to do a staged performance of *Viva Las Vegas*, the famous Elvis Presley/Ann-Margret movie musical from MGM. She wondered if I'd be interested in playing the romantic foil/bad guy, Count Elmo Mancini.

Now, I liked and respected my friend greatly. I also thought she was off her rocker. First, a lesbian-drag version of an Elvis Presley movie musical? It didn't exactly sound like a hit. Second, how and where the hell in Manhattan was she going to stage and produce it? And third, I was a classically trained theater actor, don't cha know? I did Shakespeare, I did Tennessee Williams, I did Joe Orton! I was *the* Craig Archibald!

Wisely, I did not share my honest opinion with her and instead replied, "Sure, Mags, I'm there!" I believed that would be the last I'd hear of it. She

Viva Feva! Backstage with Maggie Moore. The Cucaracha Theater, New York City, 1995.

asked me if I'd like to produce it with her and I begged off saying I was too busy (um, waiting tables).

Three months later, the phone rang. God bless Maggie if she hadn't found a theater space, a band, a director, and a cast ready to go into rehearsal in early 1995. Was I still in? Cornered (and now unemployed), I grudgingly committed to the project.

The rehearsal process was abysmal. I was horrified. I didn't understand "camp" humor and was not as amused as my costars. Rather, I was bemused. Plus, the Cucaracha Theater lived up to its name—no heat, and cockroaches underfoot. We rehearsed in winter parkas, huddled around broken space heaters.

The weeks dragged on in misery for me as I watched Maggie confidently produce the hell out of the show. As soon as we wrapped a rehearsal, I was out the door. Maggie stayed behind and continued to put the pieces in place.

At long, miserable last, we arrived at our first preview audience. I invited some actor pals to ease me through what I thought for certain would be a catastrophe extraordinaire. We hit the stage with the opening number and, much to my astonishment, the place went bananas. I was chagrined. Surely it was just a friendly reaction from our pals supporting us.

Julie Wheeler, in the role of Lucky Jackson, and I began the first scene, and when Maggie made her entrance as Rusty Martin, the reaction, again, was remarkable. It was such pandemonium that I actually stopped performing and looked at the audience like they were insane. There, in the front corner, were my three friends laughing and applauding louder than anyone else.

I was stupefied. Slowly, as we continued to roars of laughter after ovations, I suddenly saw the genius that was and is Maggie Moore. By the time we hit the finale, there wasn't a doubt in anyone's mind that we'd hit a Vegas jackpot! Afterward, I could see the jealousy in my actor-friends' eyes.

After the adoring crowd and our fellow cast members departed, I lingered at my dressing table, down the row of light bulbs from Maggie. She turned and looked at me with a cocky smile. "Now do you get it, kid?"

I blushed with more than a little shame. "I'm such an asshole."

"An asshole in a big hit!" Maggie smiled.

"How can I help you, producer lady?" I asked.

She laughed and said, "Finally! You get it! Help me, honey, we have so much to do before opening night!"

I gave Maggie all the help I could from that point on until closing night. And in doing so I learned firsthand how to produce not just a play, but an event. *Viva Las Vegas: The Musical* ran at the Cucaracha Theater, in Soho, for the remainder of 1995. It was a critical hit. Audiences packed the house. Celebrities visited us backstage and took us out to the Odeon for midnight dinners. Of all my work in the New York theater, it remains my favorite experience and memory.

Oh, and by the way—Maggie got a huge deal with ABC Television, who bought her out exclusively for the following pilot season. She established herself as a downtown diva and went on to work with New York filmmakers like John Cameron Mitchell, Tim Blake Nelson, and Todd Solondz. She has the true spirit of a self-made entrepreneur.

As for me, not only did I get the best front-seat ride onstage with Maggie and Julie; I also learned the meaning of making it happen yourself. To top it off, I got a better agent, which led to my first studio movie.

Maggie was another person who made me understand—and taught me—this invaluable lesson: you have to make it happen.

My First Three Attempts

Maggie had inspired me to make my own career happen. But the question was, how? We didn't have the digital cameras available now, so making a short film to show my talents would have been exorbitant.

I decided to write a play. I had never written one before, but I had worked tirelessly as a young actor analyzing scripts, learning scene structure, and memorizing dialogue. I figured that was enough to get me started.

My first play, *Red River*, took about a year to write. It was terrible. I mounted it for one night at the Westbeth Theatre Center on Bank Street in the West Village of Manhattan. Ten minutes into the performance, I knew it was a stinker, so I stopped, looked at the audience made up of my brave friends and family, and with a little shrug said, "This sucks." They gave me a hearty laugh of agreement, to which I replied, "I will meet you in the bar." That got me a standing (and exiting) ovation.

Writing from my heart. My fourth play, *Private Life* in my beloved Surf City, Long Beach Island, New Jersey, 1997.

My second play, *Void Where Prohibited*, took another year to birth. It was produced at HERE on lower Sixth Avenue in Soho and it was—OK. Certainly not good. But at least both the audience and I made it through without quitting or needing a drink.

My third play, *Far from the Happening Crowd*, was an entertaining evening of my personal stories from the fringes of fame and celebrity. It celebrated many close brushes with the famous, where my naive Canadian farm-boy mentality made frequent social errors. For example, the time I asked Ralph Lauren what he did for a living. True story.

Many people enjoyed the evening, but it was more memoir than play so it had limited potential for success. I knew I was improving but I also knew I needed to go deeper. The great change in my writing career happened when I learned to write from my true self and life experience.

The Essential You

One of the biggest challenges I faced as a young actor was homophobia. As a gay actor in the mid-1990s, I found the stigma of homosexuality almost reason enough to end an attempt at an acting career. Happily, it seems we are slowly moving past this era of intolerance, but when I was a young gay actor in New York City, things were difficult.

I was fortunate to be cast in one of the first small gay films produced by a major studio. Paramount Pictures produced *Kiss Me, Guido* in 1997. Several other actors in the film, also gay, and I debated and analyzed the dangers and positives of embracing our true selves in our work.

What anybody, actor or not, does in the bedroom is their own business and should have no effect on how their work is accepted. Hollywood, though, produces content for major global markets, and parts of the world are still not kind and accepting of my LGBTQIA+ family, even to this day. Back then, this was enough of a concern for many of my friends that they decided to publicly hide their sexuality.

In 1997, I began work on my fourth play, a biographical piece about a morning in the life of the British bon vivant, master playwright, and performer Noël Coward. My play essentially outed the famously closeted homosexual writer.

At the same time, I embraced myself as a gay actor. I decided that my success would not be measured by acceptance in the larger industry, and that I would rather measure my success on my personal journey of love and celebration of my essential self, my true voice.

That play changed my life.

The *New York Times*

My play, *Private Life*, opened in February 1998. The *New York Times* did not attend opening night. They weren't certain I was worth the effort until the *New York Post*, the *Daily News*, and the *Village Voice* all gave me glowing reviews. I was actually relieved that I had a week of performances before the *Times* showed up—it gave me time to get in my groove.

Show up the *Times* finally did, in the person of D. J. R. Bruckner. Backstage before the performance, knowing that Bruckner was in attendance, I suffered one of the worst attacks of nerves in my life. I'd never been one to feel nauseated before a performance, but that night I was ready to lose my lunch right up to the moment the house lights went down.

I focused on my work, turned the nerves into positive energy, and threw myself into the show. Focused and free, I went into the zone. It all went swimmingly well until, near the end of the performance, I had to perform the rather tricky physical activity of getting dressed in a 1938-style pin-striped suit, along with socks, shoes, and tie, all while talking on the phone with Marlene Dietrich.

Suddenly, in the middle of the physical feat, I realized that one of my suspenders had accidentally gotten between my legs. It was a total screwup and I had no choice but to take a moment—step out of my trousers, move the suspender to its proper position, and step back into my pants.

Promotional still, as Noël Coward in the original New York production of *Private Life*, 1998. PHOTO BY JIM MEACCI.

Knowing that my timing of the phone call was now off, I had to ad-lib dialogue to add a few precious moments to reset the timing of the costume change.

Out of my deep preparation came the confidence to say on the phone, "Oh darling, I've made a complete mess of my pants—"

The audience laughed, which gave me a few seconds to adjust and move, and to register Marlene on the other end of the line. I took one more moment for a beat, grimaced distastefully, and said, "No darling, not that kind of mess."

The audience laughed harder. And Bruckner gave me a kind and constructive review in the *New York Times*.

8
Secrets of Success

The Archibald Workbook

I came up with this idea after I'd been disappointed by a client's performance in one of his first feature films. He played the same emotional note throughout the entire film. To help him, I created what I call the Archibald Workbook, a private book meant for keeping all your notes about the film or television show you're creating in one place.

Buy a blank notebook, preferably one with a cover that endorses the spirit of the script in some way. Make the opening page include both the movie's title and the event of the movie for the character you're playing. For example, the movie's title could be *The Kidnapping* with the character subtitle reading "In which my character takes action to find his son and, in doing so, becomes his own man." The title should have meaning and clarity.

Turn that first page. You now have two blank pages staring at you. On the left page, in the top left corner, put the number 1. This is your first scene in this film. At the top right of the left-hand page, put the proper scene number as listed in the film script. For example, your first scene might actually be Scene Five in the script, so my left page at the top will show 1 and 5. (Don't include script page numbers; these change frequently.)

Below those numbers, list your answers to the two most important questions:

One. What is my action?

Two. What do I need from the other character's eyes?

Add any notes from your homework that you feel are of vital importance to the scene. For example, in creating an arc to your character's emotional life through the film, you may have decided that the happiness level of your character in the scene is a five out of ten. You may have decided this because in the next scene, your character is ten out of ten happy.

You don't want to repeat any emotion at a similar pitch to the previous scene. That's where the term "one note" comes from. By recording your scenes in one book, you make certain you can create an emotional arc to the character you're playing.

On the right page, put the same numbers in the top corners—1 and 5. This page is for notes on what actually happened while shooting the scene. Did you need to play the character's happiness at a seven? Make a note to avoid playing the same intensity level anywhere near that scene. I also keep notes of blocking (or any notes from the director about my character or about the film).

This page becomes a golden guide to reshoots. On almost every film, there are reshoots. It's a huge help to open your workbook to the scene you're reshooting and refer to the notes you made.

Turn the page and add your second-scene notes. On the left go the pre-shooting notes. On the right are your post-shooting notes.

As you go through the process of shooting, this book becomes invaluable. Shooting schedules can change overnight or with the weather. Instead of trying to recall mental notes you'd made in your homework about the scene you are unprepared to shoot, you go to your workbook for a refresher.

A client of mine shot a major guest star spot on a police procedural. Her character was kidnapped and tortured throughout the script. The makeup and hair people were delighted that she was able to tell them, "I have the black eye, but I don't have the scars yet."

Another client impressed the crew when he read aloud the exact blocking of the camera and the actors for an intricately choreographed scene they had to reshoot due to a faulty boom mic.

One final secret to the Archibald Workbook: Turn the book upside down and work from the back page toward the front, putting all your private character notes, questions, and substitutions (or at least hints to what you used for your substitution, so that no one can read the workbook and embarrass you) into the book. Now all your work is in one place.

Several clients have told me that the workbook is their on-set Bible. It's a survival guide, a form of insurance, and after you've finished shooting, it becomes a wonderful keepsake and reminder of your work.

Stage vs. Screen

One of the big challenges for actors who've been trained on the stage is the switch to camera acting. The stage and the cinema are different beasts, and you must know the differences between them.

The stage actor is the storyteller. You must get out on that stage and—along with the rest of the cast, and with the help of a few props, lights, sound cues, and set pieces—grab the attention of the audience, settle them down, and take them on the ride of the play. You must make certain they understand plot points or setups for jokes. It's your job to be the storyteller, and you need to be trained for the stage by a good university, theater school, or conservatory program to do it well.

On screen, you're no longer the storyteller. In film, that's the director's job. On television, that task falls to the executive producer/creator/showrunner. The difference is immense. The screen actor has room to relax into the character, to simply do the homework and be.

The other major difference is the proximity of the audience. On stage, your audience is at least ten to fifteen feet away. On camera, they're no more than ten to fifteen feet away. And in a close-up, the audience is less than a foot away. Imagine someone standing twelve inches in front of your face, looking directly into your eyes. How much "telling" or "showing" do you have to do for them to see your thoughts? (Answer: None!)

Yet another major difference is the volume of sound you must produce. In the theater, you must be loud and clear and clean. You must project—even in a "stage whisper"—so that the audience can hear you. You must articulate and project enough to be heard in the back row. You must train your voice for the stage, using diaphragmatic breathing, to generate the volume, and your speaking tools (tongue, lips, soft palate, vocal chords) to enunciate clearly.

In screen work, you generally have a lavalier (body) microphone pinned into your collar. Often, that mic is closer to your larynx than your ears are. And don't forget that big furry boom mic above your head or sneaking in at your knees—that thing can hear your heartbeat.

There are other smaller, nuanced differences that take time to finesse, like the placement of your eyes. An actor who works on screen learns the importance of keeping the eyes closer to the camera. On camera, you have an audience of one. You must make certain that audience sees your experience. You allow the camera to see into the back of your eyes to your character's soul. Thus, you must keep your eyes in the vicinity of the camera without looking at it. This is a particular skill that can only be learned through doing. It's subtle and takes finesse.

In a close-up on film, your off-camera scene partner generally has their eyes as close to the camera lens as possible. This allows the camera to see deep into your open and vulnerable heart. If you believe you are the character, and you're living truthfully as the character, so will your audience.

When anger or rage is called for onstage, you go "up and out" with your emotions. In film and television work, you go "down and in." Going down and in becomes especially important in self-tapes, which are often recorded on low-quality cameras and microphones. Keeping the performance intimate and cinematic makes you more professional.

To make a stage actor aware of all these differences, there's usually a retraining process. It doesn't take terribly long, but it must be done. These differences are why I don't train actors in a theater setting. When an actor trained for the stage gets up on a black stage, with seats out in the dark, they revert to their instinct to "project." Hollywood acting coaches who work out of theater spaces to teach screen acting confuse the hell out of me—and, I suspect, their clients.

Two actors who perfectly understand the transition from stage to screen are Frank Langella and Maggie Smith. He's a four-time Tony Award winner who was also nominated for an Oscar for his work in *Frost/Nixon*. She's won almost every award under the sun, most recently for her work in *Downton Abbey*. Both have mastered the art of acting in theater and cinema. That can't be said of every actor.

Preparation

Preparation is the key to success. The Archibald Questions section of chapter 3 are really just the beginning of the work. There's no end to the questions you can ask about the character you're playing and the circumstances in which they live.

That's why every actor should constantly be in class. If you aren't working out the muscles of your skill set regularly, you'll find it difficult to prove yourself when you get your opportunity. Golf tournaments are held on weekends. What do you think golfers do on weekdays before and after tournaments?

They work on different aspects of their game: driving, putting, pitching out of sand traps.

Work on your acting game and go deep. Plow the depths of your character's fertile soil! Connect deeply to the character on every level and in every way you can—from their deep psychosis to their morning beverage, from their family history to their favorite music, from their spiritual peaks to their darkest secrets.

When you walk onto a set, the entire production has put their faith in your capacity to bring your good, vulnerable, and deeply crafted portrayal to the shoot. It's your job to be completely prepared, so that you can be technically precise, emotionally spontaneous, completely in the moment, in a constant state of discovery.

State of Discovery

All the skills and ideas I'm suggesting are meant to help you discover a sense of freedom in your work. You want to live as the character in the same way you live as a person: in a constant state of discovery. What is the next moment going to bring?

As an actor, you should be constantly discovering anew. That goes for every take, every run-through, and every opportunity you get to do a scene. Two takes should never be the same. They can't ever be the same. Your job, I repeat, is to be in a constant state of discovery.

That was one of the Oscar-winning actor Martin Landau's perennial suggestions. I was honored to be inducted as a lifetime member of the Actors Studio by Marty, who passed away in 2017. He would invariably tell actors during his moderating sessions, "Live in a constant state of discovery."

Your character has no idea what the next line is. You do, but your character doesn't. Have fun as the character in discovery of the moment. The ability to do so is often the difference between an actor who auditions well and an actor who actually books the job.

Have you seen Margot Robbie in *I, Tonya*? She has a great time living in a constant state of discovery in that film. As does Christian Bale in *The Fighter* and many of his other film roles. Both of those brave and committed artists know how to let go when the camera rolls and just discover, discover, discover.

Don't Be Afraid to Be Wrong

An important element to being a true professional is irradicating the fear of making mistakes. Do not be afraid of being wrong. An excessive fear of failure or error blocks the free and natural instincts you will need in your performance. Give yourself the freedom to fuck it up. Surprisingly, when you do, you are far less likely to fuck up.

Martin Landau had great advice for this. He would say, "Try to be bad," which is a funny kind of reverse psychology. But it works. And in the rehearsal hall, "trying to be bad" may lead to some terrific discoveries you would never find otherwise.

My sister is a vice president of a large Canadian fashion company. She surprised me by telling me that they often encourage their staff to "fail fast." Their strategic thinking is that if you are going to try something that could possibly fail, do it quickly so that you get to the success sooner. I love this for our world too.

When you are wrong or fail fast—admit it. Practice the integrity of accepting responsibility and you will be amazed at how fast your good moral code rebounds to service you in the most unpredictable and positive ways. Integrity brings integrity.

Don't Be Afraid to Think

One day, Philip Seymour Hoffman invited me to lunch. We talked about how people learn to act, and I asked him: "If you had one note to give to my acting clients, what would it be?"

He gave it a good fifteen seconds of thought before replying, "Don't be afraid to think."

I loved that note, especially from him. If you watch his film performances, you'll notice that he was never afraid to think in character. He took the time to process information, or to make a decision. He didn't rush. He took his time and was not afraid to think on camera. It was part of his genius.

Remember that we're talking here about the character thinking—not you, the actor. You need to be so thorough in your homework, so deeply associated with the character, that when it comes time to process a thought, you truly take the time to honestly think it through in character. You, the actor, are not there; this is not actorbation. The character is there, in the moment of discovery, having to process their thoughts.

A client shooting a movie had a climactic scene that was extremely emotional. It was difficult for her not to make an appointment. When it came time to shoot the scene, she became self-conscious about needing to instantly access intense emotion and got locked up.

She told me she remembered Phil's note—"Don't be afraid to think"— and used that advice to stay in the moment and process her character's thoughts. The director thought it was brilliant that she chose thinking as her starting point, rather than rushing into the emotional fireworks. And the emotional fireworks, magically, now came naturally.

When we are in the moment of discovery, what we are actually doing is appraising. Human beings appraise the situation, the events, and what is being said as it happens. We should as well when acting a role.

I love Mahershala Ali's "thinking" in his performances. His characters always have deep running rivers, and he's never afraid to take the time to let his characters think. You'll see what I mean if you pay close attention to his work in Barry Jenkins's 2016 masterwork *Moonlight*.

Those Who Go Deepest, Win

One reason Michael Phelps won all those gold medals at the Olympic Games was that he always stayed in the pool the longest at practice. He worked the hardest. He gave up everything in his youth to be the best swimmer in the world. Ditto Tiger Woods as a child playing golf. Or Wayne Gretzky spending endless hours skating and stickhandling on the backyard ice rink his father built every winter.

How do you do this as an actor? Continually return to your homework—in particular, the most important questions—and make certain you've connected the answers to the core of your humanity. Then do it again. Then again. And again.

Constance Wu in *Crazy Rich Asians*. Those who go deepest, win.

In my experience, the actor who comes into the audition with the character most truthfully and deeply connected to their soul is the actor who gets the job. Let's be honest: Now and then external factors win the day. Somebody's son or niece or lover will get the job. But the actor who came in deeply connected will have won the room, and—as long as they maintain the deep integrity of their work—they'll be invited back.

Part III
THE BUSINESS

9
The Ten Business Questions

These questions are meant to get you started as an entrepreneur. You need to be the best businessperson you can be. Start at the beginning and make certain there is integrity to your business acumen so that you are centered and grounded in your work as someone in the business of acting.

1. What Is the Name of Your Company?

When you succeed in this industry, you will begin to make money. Once you have a certain income, your financial advisers will advise you to incorporate. When you incorporate, you'll need a business name.

Create that business name right now. Make it something personal and important to you. Make a list of possibilities, take your time, and make sure the name you select is one you'll be happy with for the rest of your life.

Center yourself. Go to a beach or the desert or a mountaintop. Name your company from your center, your soul. Make it something you'll be proud of. Then check and see if someone else already owns the name! Is the URL available? Do it today, before your career takes off, so that you've already established in your heart that you're an entrepreneur running a successful company.

2. What Is Your Company's Mission Statement?

Write a mission statement. It should be brief—a couple of sentences at most—and declare what you're trying to achieve.

Describe your mission.

3. What Is Your Purpose Statement?

A purpose statement should focus on the deeper motivations for your company. It can be more detailed. It should include how you're going to achieve your goals, what your success will look like, and what you're going to do with your success. It should declare your purpose on this planet.

When you're successful, you can help others. Simply putting your name on a fundraising lunch or a golf outing can add cachet and increase attendance and raise more money for the charity. How great is that? Success gives you the capacity to put that success into action.

Success in the entertainment industry can help you create wonderful charitable possibilities—whether around human rights, animal cruelty, human diseases such as cystic fibrosis, HIV-AIDS, cancer, addiction, or anything else that may speak to you. Create your company with those goals in mind. It provides a terrific foundation for future success.

And by the way, when you walk into an audition with higher goals than getting the part, they can tell; they may not know exactly what makes you centered and grounded, but they will sense that you're a person of substance with more in their vision than red carpets and a star embedded on a sidewalk.

4. What Is Your "Why"?

Why are you doing this? Why are you spending your life energy on this business?

If you understand why you're creating the business you're creating and working so diligently to become the best artist you can be, it gives you a grounded strength. And it has another benefit. As my business coach, Les McGehee, says, "If the why is big enough, the how will present itself."

5. What Are the Principles of Your Company?

You provide a service called acting. What kind of actor do you want to be? What are your principles? Are you the sort of actor who always shows up on time with your lines memorized?

As the owner of a production company, you'll be involved in producing content. What kind of content do you want to create? What kind of stories do you want to tell? How do you want to share with the world your personal beliefs?

Make a list of the principles by which you intend to run your company. You're the owner. You'll have employees. If you pay someone, they work for you. That includes me. That also includes your manager and your agent, although they don't like to think of it that way, and they have their agendas as well. At the end of the day, you pay them—they work for you. They're your staff. How are you going to treat them?

Beyond them, you will also eventually have assistants, public relations companies, financial advisers, makeup artists, housekeepers, and drivers. What kind of boss will you be?

Personally, I've worked for many horrible bosses, in restaurants and bars worldwide, and been mistreated by many business owners and managers. I vowed that I'd never treat my own staff that way.

And don't forget, in this world of social media, it is important how you present yourself, particularly in times that are professionally challenging. Make certain you do not cause irreparable harm to yourself, your company, or those you work for and with.

Add to your list of principles as you learn from your life experiences, the support jobs you have, and anything that comes your way along your career path. Be on the lookout for wonderful bosses or managers who treat people beautifully. Learn and be inspired by them.

6. What's on Your Vision List?

When I graduated from the Neighborhood Playhouse in 1989, I created a list of twenty things that would prove that I had become a successful artist. My list included things like appearing in a national tour; being in an Academy Award–winning film; and becoming a member of the Actors Studio. In the past twenty-five years, I've realized those goals, along with many others. I still have many to achieve.

One of the reasons I've achieved those things is that I made a vision list. When we articulate specific goals, our subconscious takes on the assignment and makes subtle choices along the way to help us achieve them. We take actions that support our aims and intentions.

So make a vision list. Don't be afraid to include the desire to win major awards. There's the teacher of the year award. Lawyer of the year. Car salesperson of the year. The Nobel and Peabody committees award outstanding work. Don't be shy about wanting to win an Oscar or an Emmy. They represent a tremendous compliment from your peers. Yes, they are also highly political, but in their essence, they're voted for by your fellow artists and intended as recognition for outstanding work. Champions win awards. Or at least get nominated.

7. What's Your Five-Year Plan?

Think about where you want to be in five years. Go for it—don't be afraid to challenge yourself. Envision what you'd be happy doing five years from now. Be specific. Be detailed. See it clearly. Imagine the life you wish to be living.

That vision will give you a distant point of reference to aim for. It will also give you a sort of work-back schedule. If your goal five years from now is to be a regular on an Emmy award–winning television series, certain things need to happen between now and then.

Four years from now, the show will be in production. Three years from now, that show will be a pilot in which you're cast. Two years from now, you'll need to be well known in the casting offices of the television channels.

This means that one year from now, you need management and agency teams able to get you in the door of the best casting directors so that you can begin to show your high-quality work and they can trust you to be good in the room when they take you to the producers of the pilots.

List all the things you need to do to accomplish your goals. Listing tasks and priorities allows you to keep track of your forward progress while inspiring you to execute necessary tasks in the appropriate order. A Harvard University study found that people who make lists earn, on average, ten times more than those who don't. Need any more motivation?

As your five-year plan unfolds, other opportunities may well come into play. You're not going to reject things that can move you toward your goals; however, you must stay open to possibilities that may not fit into the vision. You never know what's going to happen or exactly how it's going to happen.

When you have specific goals, they inspire you to take action. And action—not wishing, or hoping, or empty fantasizing—is ultimately what produces results.

8. What's Your Crisis Management Plan?

All businesses need a crisis management plan. A sneaker company may have its laces made in a factory in Guatemala. The company will have a backup plan to source laces elsewhere in case an earthquake or political rebellion hits Guatemala. The company will also have a backup plan should there be disruption of their work at their offices in the United States. All businesses have contingency and crisis-management plans. Your business needs one, too.

Artists can go into crisis when they receive a devastating comment from a friend, family member, or the *New York Times*. Or when they get edited out of a movie. Or when their agency drops them, or when the part they were promised is taken away. The death of a loved relative or friend, a relationship gone sour, a car accident—personal issues can strike without warning and precipitate a crisis.

That's why you need a plan. Look at your life and figure out how you can best help yourself. Know yourself as the entrepreneur, the artist, and the private individual. Learn how you can best rebound from problems or crises.

Personally, I rebound with a call to my business coach, or taking a walk around the block, or recalling the days when I worked as a waiter. That last memory is enough to shock me out of any kind of self-pity and into my power. I also head to the movies. Popcorn, Raisinets, and a root beer soothe the worst blues. A personal crisis is best managed with massage, music, meditation, yoga, and a visit to a special Malibu beach.

Make your crisis management plan. In tough times, it helps you make everything make you better.

9. How Do You Spend Your Down Time?

What to do when you have nothing to do? How do you take care of yourself when you have a break in your schedule? Between gigs, how do you use your time to both rest and take care of yourself and get ready for the next job? Do you invest in an action that gives back to others? Do you use that time and energy to create a family life, or enrich your friendships? The last thing I ever want to hear is, "I have nothing to do." Those words, from a client, drive me crazy.

10. What Are You Doing to Self-Create?

Do you create works of art yourself? Movies? Web series? Are you writing and producing a short film? Most successful people in Hollywood do multiple jobs at once. They act, write, produce, and direct. Everything feeds everything else. When you have a steady gig on a television show, that's a lovely time to not just work hard on a show but also plan and create your own future projects.

Getting my entrepreneurship on. Filming videos for the Archibald Studio's YouTube Channel, 2019.

10

The Audition

Understanding the Casting Process

Many actors fundamentally misunderstand the casting process. It's important that you do not.

Imagine there's a jewelry store in a shopping center like the Grove or the Beverly Center. The store specializes in renting out fantastic, uniquely designed jewelry for special events.

In walks a client. "Hi, I'd like to rent a necklace for a red-carpet event. It's an MTV party. I need classic and elegant, but with a bit of flair."

With my fellow Actors Studio warriors, Brian Foyster and Kevin Stapleton, Los Angeles, 2001.

The sales associate says, "Oh, I've got several pieces I think you'll like!" She returns with ten exquisite necklaces. Each has its own special qualities.

The client looks at all ten and sets seven of them aside as not quite right. The decision has nothing to do with how great each necklace is, and everything to do with the specifics of the event. Some of the necklaces were a bit too showy. Those went back in the display case for the next client. Neither the client nor the sales associate judged those necklaces negatively—they were all of high quality—they just didn't suit the occasion.

The client takes the three necklaces into the dressing room and closely examines each of them, finally deciding that the diamond-and-emerald piece is perfect. All the necklaces were lovely; this one just happened to be best for the event and the leading lady who was going to wear it. The necklace would make both her and the jewelry store look good.

The client is the producer. The sales associate is the casting director. And you, my dear actors, are the gems.

Casting offices want you to be of high quality and perfectly suited to the role. They want you to be the best you can be. As an actor, you have the power to make them look good to the producers and directors and networks who will hire them again to cast their projects. It's all about reputation—theirs and yours. Your value as an actor depends in large part on how good you make them look.

No one has job security in Hollywood. Everyone, even the studio head, is insecure. Casting directors are just like everyone else; they have to land the next gig. The top casting directors are the ones with the best pool of talent: actors who never let them down. If you're a solid actor—trustworthy, always prepared, in the moment, off script, and ready to go—you'll be adored by the casting directors.

Planting a Garden in Hollywood

Here's how the casting process works. An agent or manager sees a perfect role for one of their new actors in the breakdown service. She calls up the casting director and says, "You've got to see this actor!"

The casting director says, "Are you sure? Please don't waste my time!"

And the agent says, "Believe me. This kid is great. You've got to see them!"

The casting director gives the actor an appointment for a pre-read. The actor comes in for the audition and is wonderful. Fully prepared. Off book. Emotionally available. Connected with the reader. Vulnerable. And yes, a good actor.

The casting director says to the actor, "Good job!"

The actor leaves thinking, "Yes! I nailed it!"

The casting director calls the agent and says, "You were right, they were great! But they aren't going any further. I can only take the best to this director, and I can't trust your actor yet, because I haven't seen them enough. My reputation is on the line with this director, so just know that they did great and I'll see them again for future projects."

The agent relays this good message to the actor. The actor is confused. They thought they'd done wonderfully. And they had. The casting director has to be able to trust that the actor will not let them down. The actor is disappointed, not realizing they've planted a beautiful seed.

A month later, the casting director is casting another project, remembers that wonderful actor, and calls them in for an audition. The actor nails it again. The casting director is delighted to have found a talented artist who can be trusted to be good in the room.

The casting director calls the agent and says, "They got a callback—let's take them to the producers."

The actor is stoked! They go to the callback for the producer and nail it again. The casting director is delighted. The producer turns to the casting director and says, "They were great, but we aren't going any further—my reputation is on the line with the network, so I can only take the best to network and I can't trust your actor yet."

The message gets relayed. Again, the actor is confused. They thought they'd killed it, and indeed they had. But the producer can't put his reputation with the network at stake by bringing in an unproven talent. Again, the actor doesn't realize the great seed they've planted with the producer.

A year goes by. The casting director and the producer are working on another project together. This time, the casting director calls the actor straight into the producer session. No pre-read. The actor comes in and again proves how talented they are and nails it beautifully.

This time the producer jumps up from behind the table and says, "Great! We're taking you to the network!"

Fantastic! Everyone is happy! The producer, casting director, agent/manager, actor, mom, and dad.

The actor goes into the network session and does their job; they live truthfully as that character under the imaginary circumstances; they are alive and in the moment; there is no bullshit or "acting"; they are funny and vulnerable and real. They kill it!

The network executive turns to the producer and casting director and says, "Great job. But they aren't going any further—I can't trust them with a $100 million television show. I can only trust the best, and I don't know them well enough yet."

Sorry to disappoint you or sound negative, but this is how the casting process works. It's all about reputation. And everyone is concerned, first and foremost, with their own!

Is it possible that a young actor could skip up that ladder of experience faster? Of course, it happens all the time. But as a coach preparing young actors for this industry, I try to keep my clients firmly grounded in reality. For most of your first few years in the industry, you'll be going from casting office to casting office, planting seeds of trustworthy work. Over time, the seeds will grow. Each visit to the office is an opportunity to water and fertilize the beautiful, blossoming tree you've planted.

Over the years, if you work hard and maintain the integrity of a quality artist, you'll plant a garden of gorgeous trees in Los Angeles, New York, and around the world.

A Day in the Life

One of Hollywood's great illusions is disguising the fact that making film and television is grunt work. People imagine it's glitz and glamour, red carpet, lipstick, tuxedos, limousines. No. It is, for the most part, blue-collar work. There's hardly anyone working on a film or television set who isn't physically exhausted by the end of the day.

Let's look at the day of an executive producer/showrunner. Let's call this fantasy character Tommy Galiano. Tommy rises early, at 5:00 a.m. He jumps on his stationary bike for a half-hour before hopping in the shower, downing a healthy breakfast, and getting out the door by 6:00 a.m.

At 6:30 a.m. he arrives at the studio. There, he meets with his top creative team. They go over the day's event schedule, looking at every possible problem they may have to address before they head off to conquer the day.

By 7:00 a.m., the entire staff has arrived to go about the business of making a hit television series. Tommy starts in the writers' room. There, he spends an hour going over everything the writers need to discuss. Dialogue issues with tomorrow's major courtroom scene. Problems in the story arc for episode four. Two of the top writers are fighting, and he has to speak to them individually to mend fences.

At 8:00 a.m., he's down on the set making certain that the day begins on time. He checks in with his director, his camera crew, and his leading cast members before he is off to the production-editing base.

And so his day proceeds, hour by hour, department by department, problem solving, creative planning, and managing logistics.

At noon, Tommy's in a meeting with the top brass at HBO, who are not only concerned about last week's numbers but also want to buy the next film he's in talks to develop.

The afternoon is spent back on the set, back up to the writers' room, the costume department, and the production design office, where they've found out that next week's plan to shoot in a local restaurant will be impossible because the health board has closed the restaurant.

Finally, at the end of the day, he arrives at the casting office. He's exhausted, his head is spinning. He has a quick espresso to wake up and be available to the actors coming to the audition. He arrives a moment or two late. Hurrying through the office, he scrambles to the desk and sits, awaiting the first of the actors the casting directors have chosen to be seen in this producer session.

At that point, in walks an actor with an attitude.

It could be the "victim" attitude. Or the "needy" attitude. How about the "over it" attitude. Or the "too cool for school" attitude. Or the "please validate my entire life" attitude. Or, perhaps worst of all, the "I'm a fucking star, damn it" attitude.

Can you imagine how much Tommy Galiano wants to kill that actor? Can you imagine, after that exhausting day, having to babysit somebody with serious attitude?

Now imagine a confident actor. Someone who doesn't need hand holding. Someone completely prepared and ready to work. Someone who brings the character to life with their heart and soul. Someone who will be a professional on the set and will need nothing more than an opportunity to work.

Guess which kind of actor gets cast.

The Day of the Audition

Decide that everything that happens prior to the audition is going to help enrich the character you're playing. The character is going to the gym. The character is getting into the shower. The character discovers a blemish on their nose. The character gets a flat tire. Well, how would the character deal with a flat tire? Use it all to make you better.

It's helpful to anticipate any possible problems and prepare yourself with the knowledge that you can use those problems to your advantage. For example, there could be a really bad reader in the audition. Use that to illuminate the other character in the scene. It's your partner who's so mad at you she can't be bothered to look you in the eye. Or so shy she's having a hard time saying her words—and that's not off-putting, it's beautiful!

Nothing's going to throw you off because you're prepared for anything and determined to use whatever circumstances you encounter to make yourself better. This way of thinking will promote you into a place of confident wholeness and reality. We're all human. We all make mistakes. We all have tension. We all have issues. This is about using the energy around you, no matter how toxic it may seem, to make you better. Take perceived obstacles and turn them into opportunities.

It's Not Your Job to Be a Good Actor

When you go into an audition, it's not your job to be a good actor. I'm going to say it again so you really understand this important note. Understanding it can change your career. It's not your job to be a good actor.

It is also not your job to:

Be sexy.

Be funny.

Be smart.

Be manly.

Be feminine.

Be cute.

Be entertaining.

Seek validation.

Get approval.

Receive good feedback.

Start deep friendships.

Prove you've done your homework.

Show your homework.

Convince people how uniquely talented you are.

None of that matters at all. None of that is your job.

What is your job?

It's your job to be the character. That's it. Just be the character.

Go into the room. Be a pro. Be considerate. Connect with the reader or your fellow actor, and be the character, living truthfully in the moment, off book, not acting, not bullshitting, not performing. Truthfully connect with, and react to, the reader or your fellow actor. Show them who you will be on set. Who you will be on the set is the character. That's your job.

Then go home without seeking approval. When you are up for a role, it's a great idea to do as much daydreaming about NOT getting it as you do about getting it.

If you simply are the character, truthfully, then you will be good, you will be funny, you will be sexy and charming. You'll receive validation and positive feedback and approval. You might even get a callback or, even better, book the job.

One of the secrets of this industry is this: People are looking to hire actors who understand how the system works. Who don't need to be taken care of or babied. Who know that their job isn't to be a "good actor," but simply to be the character.

The String Metaphor

Let's imagine there is a loose thread on the leg of my trousers. I want to get it off my pants, so I try to push it toward my knee. When I do that, what happens to the string? It gets all bunched up, crinkled under my fingers, until I finally reach my knee and push the now knotted and clumped up string over the edge. This is messy and annoyingly difficult.

This is what happens in an audition if you are thinking the wrong thoughts. If you are "trying to be good," "trying to do the part 'right,'" or "trying to get the part." You are pushing the string in the wrong direction. It is messy and difficult.

If I simply grab the end of the string nearest to me on my lap and give it a pull, the string comes off easily.

This is what happens when you are in an audition and thinking the correct way—when you are completely committed to the integrity of the character you are playing. You aren't worried about the outcome. You are the character under the circumstances. You are doing the job they are looking for you to do.

It's all about your mindset. Pull the string.

Nerves

One of the biggest impediments to a successful audition is nervousness. Nerves can throw you down, squash you, kill your focus, and cause you to bomb. So how do you make a bad case of nerves make you better?

It's rare that a writer creates a scene with no tension. And where there's tension there is nervous energy. If you can find a way to take the energy of your own nerves and transfer them to your character, your emotional preparation is easy. Those dreaded nerves become a truthful emotion in your corner.

If you pre-think it, you can usually find a way to use any number of possible energies and emotions to your advantage. Can you see why your character would be feeling judged, the way you feel in the audition room? You have the power to use your creativity to turn any event around.

Ultimately, it's about allowing yourself to be human. It's human and inevitable for things to go wrong. That human quality is exactly what they're looking for in the audition room. They're not looking for a "good actor"; they're looking for the actor who understands that the job is to simply be the character.

The more you practice it, the more you realize that your humanity is what makes you better, because it makes you real. You're just a human being, and that brings you closer to the work.

Feeling Judged

The truth is that in an audition, you are being judged. You're being watched and adjudicated in a selective process. How can this make you better? Well, most characters in most scenes sense that they're being judged, either by the other characters or by society in general.

If you feel a block or resistance in the moment of performance, it's OK to accept it. People have resistance. You can simply let your reality be the characters. The essence of your experience, your lack of control over it, can be seen as a beautiful gift to make you vulnerable and human.

Do Not Practice Failing

Everyone can find a reason to fail. You're too fat or too thin. Too tall or too short, too dark or too light, or whatever makes you think you're not going to make it. Remember, though, it's exactly the things that make you different and unique that make you successful.

What you take into the audition room is what they see. Go in seeking validation, that's what they'll see. Go in nervous about your script retention, that's what they'll see. If you go in completely invested in the character and move into the moment with open human truth and vulnerability, that's what they'll see. Who do you think is going to be cast?

Be Vulnerable

Here's a simple note that most actors forget. You're playing a human being. And all human beings—even the billionaires, even the heartless creeps, even the elected bullies—are vulnerable. Many actors forget this. And because the audition process feels so incredibly judgmental, they buoy themselves by purposefully "bucking up" and fighting back their nerves and crunching down insecurities to the point that they become inhuman power balls of energy, aggressively protecting against judgment. As a result, they show no vulnerability whatsoever.

Often, it's the vulnerability of an actor's performance that attracts people. Again, your job is to get the audience to believe you are the character—to gain their trust, so that they give you their willing suspension of disbelief and go with you on the ride of the story. An artist who lacks vulnerability lacks humanity. And if you lack humanity, you're not going to be hired to play anything other than nonhumans.

You have a pimple on audition day? That makes you vulnerable. It makes you human. Vulnerability, organically channeled into your character, can bring the character to life in a beautifully human way—and be the quality in your performance that gets you the job.

Tell Yourself to Fuck Off

One feature of a good audition is that you, personally, are not there. You're not watching and judging and recording and white knuckling your work, trying desperately to hit the appointed notes and be as brilliant as you were the night before in your living room.

It doesn't work that way. You must tell yourself to fuck off. Watching yourself as you work is a huge mistake. You must learn to leave yourself alone so that you can actually do the work of being the character. Repeat: you must tell yourself to fuck off.

In acting class in New York in 1988, Robert X. Modica said to me, after a particularly heady scene, "Craig, you prick with ears, you gotta let go of your brain. It's not the best thing you've got."

I realized he was telling me I was in my head too much and that I needed to trust my heart. And I had to figure out how to do that. I began telling myself: "Craig, wait right here in the car. I'll see you after I'm done working." And then I do the job of being the character.

Don't get angry at the thoughts that interrupt your work. Getting angry is yet another distraction. Simply acknowledge that your ego brain is engaged and let it go. If you are frustrated, give that feeling to the character and let it bubble up to give the scene more life.

Figure out how you can leave your brain behind at an audition. Here's a hint: investigate your ego. Sometimes it's not your best friend. Remember, the heart gets the part.

The Launch Primer

There is an important moment often hurried past by actors, a few seconds before the scene actually begins, that space between "OK, here we go" and "Action." Sometimes (in the casting office), this period of time can be minuscule. Other times (on a set), you can be in limbo for up to a minute. I'm addressing what I like to call your launch primer. In other words, what are your actual thoughts as you wait for the moment of performance?

We see extreme examples of this in the sporting world, from basketball players' rituals at the free throw line; baseball players in the batter's box tapping the bat, practice swinging, and wiping their helmets; and tennis players bouncing, tapping, and adjusting undergear before they serve or prepare to return service. Top professionals have customized habits they have honed and perfected so that they are set up to succeed.

And so, I ask you, what do you do before the moment of performance?

Personally, I find it helpful to be in character as much as possible in the half hour leading up to work. I try to leave myself in the car or in the trailer while I, as the character, walk to the casting office or set.

I can still be "Craig" if I need to, but only a small percentage of me is available. For the most part, I am now fully committed to the character and the given circumstances from the script.

Once I've arrived at the point just prior to "Action," I have five solid steps. First, I tell what is left of Craig to fuck off. Second, I remind myself of my "trigger sentence" (the line in the script that encompasses the essence of the scene). Next, I ask and remind myself (in character), "What is my action?" Fourth, I remind myself, "What am I looking for in the other actor's eyes?" Finally, I take a deep breath to relax and focus on the moment before. When I hear "Action," I simply trust my homework and do my job of being the character.

Very often, just as we are getting settled into the launch primer, we are required to "hold" or "stand by." What you do in that holding standby is crucial. Some actors run their lines, some like to make jokes and small talk. I like to float in my launch primer—gently bouncing from question to question, staying in character and primed to launch.

What do you do to be your best when you hear "action"?

Receiving a Note from a Casting Director

The worst thing you can do when given a note from a casting director is to take it personally. Or to assume that what you just did was completely wrong. No. No. No.

Don't do this. Don't self-sabotage. Don't second-guess your good hard work. (That is, assuming you did your good hard work!)

When a casting director gives you a note, they're simply trying to guide you to your best. They could be testing you to see how you take the adjustment, so they can see you won't panic when given a note by the director or creative producer. Usually, they're guiding you toward what they know the creative team is looking for in the part.

You may see the note as "tightened tailoring," which constricts your choices and tightens you up. Better to think of it as "letting out the seams," which gives you more room, more freedom.

The casting director wants you to be good so that they look good to the creative team, get the job of casting done, get paid, and go home!

Receiving a Note from a Director or Creative Producer

If they take the time to give you a note, they're seeing something in your work that could possibly fit into their project. They're interested in seeing how you work and how you process information. They could be challenging you to see how easily you can make an adjustment. They could also be testing how self-sabotaging you are—a clear sign that you'll be difficult to work with.

A well-known television director told me over dinner that he purposely gives actors with the potential to book the job a direction that contradicts what they've been told by the casting directors or in the character description breakdown. He doesn't do this to see some new interpretation. He does it to see their note-taking process.

He will not hire an actor who beats themself up for assuming they've made a horrible mistake; that actor is going to be difficult to work with. Anyone willing to punish themself with harsh self-judgment is not attractive to work with. They're also probably green for giving up so easily on trusting their gut. If you've really done the homework, you'll be able to take a note without drama or trauma.

Many actors worry too much about "being right" or "how casting wants to see it." They make safe choices so that they don't make a mistake. The ironic thing is that trying to avoid mistakes is a major mistake!

Because so many actors do this, it's actually rare that actors bring in work with true choices. Casting people are happy when an actor actually makes a choice. It doesn't matter if it's a wrong choice—they can give you that note, and you can simply change it! But making the choice is important. Go ahead, make a choice. Make it good and complicate it with your wonderful human vulnerability. Be brave and step into your true power.

A Note to our Industry Professional Friends

Please stop the practice of asking actors to prepare three or four scenes before telling them upon arrival at the casting office that you will only see one of the scenes. This is a familiar, unfair, and selfish transgression against actors whose audition preparation time is valuable—and unpaid. A small amount of due diligence on your part would go a long way to making actors' days more manageable and ultimately give you a better performance.

And while I'm at it, when will this industry learn to give actors more than one night to prepare for an audition? This is unbelievably dumb. Hey Hollywood, you are shooting yourselves in the foot when you don't give professional artists the necessary time to be a professional artist. Not all great actors are quick studies. All actors benefit from additional time to prepare. And yes, of course, actors need to be able to be spontaneous and adapt on the fly, but that should be the exception, not the rule.

A Victory Story

One evening, in the middle of a busy pilot season, I got a call from a client asking for an emergency work session the following morning. All I had available was a half hour at 10:00 a.m.

The following morning, we dove into the audition scenes. It was a quirky one-hour script for ABC Television in a genre not easy to identify—somewhere between comedy, drama, and psychological procedural.

We had such limited time that I realized the only thing I could really do was support my client with his choices and bolster his confidence. I felt a twinge of regret because I didn't feel we actually "got" it. However, we had no choice but to soldier on. A half hour later, out the door he went, and I carried on with my appointments.

Two hours later my client started texting. "Didn't go well." "Damn!" "I'm not going further!" "This is stupid."

I texted back, "Ask your manager to get feedback."

A half hour later he texted, "They say they're looking for a Dulé Hill type. This is so stupid, I replaced him in a play in New York! I'm perfect for this!"

His disappointed texts continued through the afternoon. He was supposed to be in class that evening, but mid-afternoon he texted, "I'm so angry! I'm not going to come to class—I've got to go run this off at the beach, sorry."

I was disappointed but wished him a happy sunset run.

A half hour later he texted again: "Fuck that! I'm not going for a run. I'm coming to class and we are going to work it. And if you have time after class can we put it on tape?"

"That's my kind of champion!" I replied. "Yes, yes, and yes!"

That evening, we worked the scene for almost an hour before we finally figured out the rhythm to the words and he got the whole class laughing. We'd found it. After class, he stayed for two hours while we put it on tape. I edited and uploaded the best takes and sent the digital file to his manager at one-thirty in the morning.

The next morning my client's manager viewed our tape. She liked it and forwarded it to the casting director.

The casting director loved it! He was impressed with the second effort, and my client immediately got a call back from the producers.

The next day, he met the producers, who took him to the network. The network approved him, and my client was signed as a series regular on his first pilot for a major network.

He reached out, worked hard, and found a solution. He didn't just give up and pout. That's the spirit of a champion audition!

A Challenging Story

Several years ago, a client came to the studio to prepare for an audition, which included her character having a New Jersey accent. Sometimes I don't have time to read the breakdown for my client's auditions, and this particular morning was especially busy.

After an hour's work, she was confident and ready. We'd found a few unique and original moments, and we added a couple of "buttons" (funny punch lines) to make things pop. I thought she was in great shape. Off she went to her audition.

Several hours later, I got a call from her. She told me that she'd gone in the room centered, focused, and ready to go. She sat down in the chair, not needing a script because she was off book (as I insist all my clients be), and worked with the reader truthfully and in the moment.

When she finished, she saw that the producers were all amused. The scene was not a comedy. The showrunner/executive producer smiled at her and said, "What on God's green earth made you decide to do that with a New Jersey accent?" Naturally, my client was horrified and said, "What? It says it in the character description!"

It turned out that it did not say that. But because my client was so confident and prepared, they loved her! And they'd all had a good laugh. They asked her to do it again without the New Jersey accent. Could she add a little southern accent? She did and booked the job.

What does that say about the casting process? Mostly, it says if you're prepared and confident and available and present in the room, you can overcome any problems or mistakes. You can take any adjustments and make everything make you better. When the casting directors and producing team see that you're that kind of actor, they're more likely to hire you, even if you do make a major mistake!

An interesting footnote. That same client, several years later, went in for an audition and saw that the breakdown requested a southern accent. She prepared accordingly, worked it up with me at the studio, and went in and did a good audition. (We both double-checked that the breakdown requested a southern accent!) When she finished, the casting director said, "What on God's green earth made you decide to do that with a southern accent?"

My client was horrified and thought that she had made the same mistake again! But then the creator/producer spoke up and said to the casting director, "The breakdown says it has a southern accent, because this character has a southern accent!"—to which the horrified casting director replied, "It does?"

Some actors give the casting directors too much power. They do not hold the keys to the kingdom. They are not gods. They're simply fellow workers in an industry that can be a difficult, demanding grind. Everybody's human, everybody makes mistakes—even casting directors.

Same Story, Different Outcomes

This happened to two of my movie-star clients on the same day. When the first client arrived at the casting office on one of the big studio lots, he was horrified that the casting director had her dog in the room with her.

"Good morning," he said. ("What the fuck," he thought.)

Now this is a successful guy, and very serious. He took the dog's presence as an insult. He did his best to ignore the animal and began his audition. Unfortunately, the dog began to whine, and it barked several times during the audition. It really threw my client off his game.

The other client also had an important audition in a big-time casting office. He arrived to a room full of studio executives sitting in on his audition.

During the audition, one of the executives started texting. It threw my client off, and he could feel his anger rising. Instead of letting it get the best of him, he thought, "How can I make this work? How can I use this anger for the character right now?" So he focused his anger directly into his work as the character. He hung in, finished the scene, and did well enough to earn himself a call back.

The actor with the casting director's barking dog, however, got up and stormed out. He left the lot and could not be talked into returning.

Imagine the feedback he got at the end of the day from his manager and his agent? He vented to me on the phone that night, claiming he was making a point about respect. The bottom line is that there are now negative feelings between him and that casting director. To this day, she has not called him back in.

If he'd found some way to make that dog work for him, he would have been the bigger person, a true professional who could take a bad situation and make it work.

Similar situations, different mindsets, different outcomes.

After the Audition Is Over

Bringing in a good audition is like offering a gift. You've spent your valuable time and energy preparing. You have likely spent money getting coached before going in. You used your beautiful soul and hard-earned life experience to bring the character to life. You brought them your gift, and as with any true gift, you must offer it without any thought of return.

No amount of fretting or rerunning the audition is going to change the outcome. Learn from it, sure, but do not obsess and fester. Give them your gift, then walk away. After the audition is over, you simply have to let it go.

The Secret to Conquering Rejection

The secret to conquering rejection is to get excited about it. If you are being rejected, that means that you are actively and optimistically doing something called building your business. Rejection is a symbol of success. You are taking action. You aren't backing away from the challenge—you are facing it down like a champion. That's a great thing!

The Past Is the Past

I had a neighbor in New York City. She was an elderly lady named Mrs. Liebowitz. Mrs. Liebowitz was a character. A classic New Yorker, she was often mean, casually caustic, and always funny. I adored her. (In fact, one night I saved her life when I got home late and could smell gas coming from her apartment. The NYFD knocked down her door and saved her. I heard her complaining to them. "Oh gawd, who called you? I didn't know I left the oven on but to think I could've died and wouldn't have to deal with you!")

One day, I helped her into her apartment with her groceries. As I placed the bags inside her door and stepped out, something made me ask her, "Mrs. Liebowitz, you've seen everything life has to offer, what would you say is the secret to life?"

She looked at me with a genuine disgust and barked, "The past is the past!" She emphasized her point by slamming the door in my face!

As our old friend Anonymous stated, "Truer words were never spoken."

When the audition is over, let it go. The past is the past.

Business Mindset

John C. Maxwell

The American leadership expert John C. Maxwell wisely stated: "Learn to say 'no' to the good so you can say 'yes' to the best."

This comes in handy when you get distracted by friends and family who want your attention and focus on events, issues, or projects that don't actually help you move forward. It is OK to say "no" to people so that you can say "yes" to being your best.

Take Responsibility

As a business owner, you must take responsibility for everything. This includes mistakes that have been made by others who work for and with you. Be willing to forgive others for those mistakes. Most importantly, be willing to forgive yourself. We all make mistakes.

At the Corner of Art and Commerce

Think of the entertainment industry as a city block. We are walking down Art Avenue. As we approach Commerce Street, we are careful. It's a busy street with many large trucks that can seriously hurt us. If we turn onto Commerce Street and stay for too long, we become Instagram influencers. My clever clients wait carefully for the light to turn before crossing, taking what they need from Commerce Street, and then continuing down Art Avenue.

A Goal and a Dream

The difference between a goal and a dream is that goals have a plan. Yes, I certainly want you to believe in a dream. But don't forget to set goals around that dream. Set success criteria. Make it measurable. Set metrics around that goal. In the November 1981 issue of *Management Review*, George T. Doran sets out the classic SMART criteria for goal planning and objectives.

S = Specific
M = Measurable
A = Achievable
R = Realistic
T = Timely

Make your plans adhere to these rules and you will find them achievable.

And don't take the success criteria lightly. These are crucial to your benefits realization. In other words, you can remind yourself that you are actually succeeding when you know what success looks like.

Morning and Evening Practice

Self-care and making time for yourself is essential to your success. Creating practices that help you be your best in the morning and again before bed has made huge impacts on my clients' careers. Implementing positive health habits such as gym workouts, meditation, breathing exercises, yoga stretches, journaling, and so on can significantly improve your productivity.

Business Relationships

Friends? Not friends? Employee? Not employee? Who is who and what do they mean to you? And what about loyalty? Doesn't that count?

After years of holding my client's hands through difficult days of being dropped by their agent or manager or being cast in a film and then cut out of it, or being cast in a show and then fired, it is now abundantly clear to me that loyalty has no true value or place in business.

That might sound negative or hardened, but I've just seen too many trusting and loyal artists hurt by aggressive business types.

I'm all for being kind and loyal but only when maintaining one sober eye on performance. If someone is your business partner and they are performing up to your standards, then you should continue with them. If their performance becomes substandard, then by all means drop them and find someone better. If your performance becomes substandard, do not be surprised when they do the same.

It is important to know the difference between personal and professional relationships.

Personal relationships are based on the quality of the bond you have with the other person. It should be a mutually positive exchange built on love, support, and care for each other. The focus should be on each other's well-being. These relationships are based on intimacy, trust, and selflessness. One can trust these relationships because they are not always based on self-first thinking. The people who truly love us at times do things for our betterment before theirs.

Professional relationships may have some of the above positive qualities, but they are focused on the advancement of both parties' careers and professional goals. Usually what is at stake in these relationships is financial or reputation-based. Intimacy is not required and perhaps not even wise in this world. Trust is not something we give easily. It is earned through time.

Both relationships are fraught with the possibility of disappointment, exploitation, and jealousy. Personal revelations of this kind are easily spotted and addressed. Professional deception can be much more difficult to see and address. Don't forget that people with whom you do business are not your friends and family. They are business associates. This doesn't mean you cannot appreciate genuine, well-intentioned behavior. It just means you should never blindly or naively place your trust in a business associate. Know in your heart that they will always be looking out for themselves first.

Understanding this, you can move forward to manage these relationships with grace, dignity, and confidence.

The ancient Greek philosopher Aristotle identified three kinds of friendships. This can be a helpful common-sense guide for you in your business and personal relationships:

1. Friendship of Advantage. This is a friendship where the other person is profitable to you in some way. And very likely vice versa, you are profitable to them.

2. Friendship of Comfort. This relationship is based on someone's company or association you find pleasurable. Fun friends.

3. Friendship of Value. This is a relationship based on mutual appreciation and esteem. This type of relationship is based on agreed-upon ethics and takes longer to build.

According to Aristotle, the first two don't last as long as the third.

As long as you live within your own moral code regarding these issues, you can take whatever action you believe is best.

It is OK to have the relationship you desire with your business connections. Just don't be naive. Understand and know what kind of friend/employee/employer they truly are.

Recognizing Predators

Sadly, there are people who abuse their positions of power in our world. Thankfully, in the last few years there's been terrific movement forward to exposing inappropriate workplace behavior, particularly in the film and television industry.

That said, there are, and probably always will be, predators willing to take a chance on their reputation to gain a sexual advantage. Do not be naive. This happens to men as well as women. Do not ever think that being sexually active with a person will help your career. It won't. Maintain your integrity to yourself at all costs and insist that industry professionals approach you professionally.

11

The Boring
(But Important) Shit

Many actors—artists of all stripes—get turned off as soon as the discussion turns to the business side of their business. So if you're still reading this, well done! Business expertise often separates the gonnabes from the wannabes.

You're running a business and need to know that business inside and out. Read industry books, blogs, newspapers, and magazine articles. Ask questions at seminars and workshops. Investigate the ins and outs of being a working actor. Ask for guidance from people you trust. Be discerning as you gain knowledge and get better at evaluating advice.

I once had a client say, "I have nothing to do! I'm so bored! I go to class, I work out, I go to auditions when I get them, but there's not much more for me to do." I told her she could create short films, watch Oscar performances, or do business reading. "Oh, but that's so boring!" she said. It should come as no surprise that she is now a restaurant manager.

Contracts

I used to be a horrible businessperson myself. It wasn't until I woke up and saw my friends succeeding that I realized that if I didn't get wise, I would never join them.

I happened into a part-time job working for a lawyer. One of my first tasks was reading contracts. The lawyer wanted me to get acclimated to the world I'd be working in. I sat down with a contract and began to read it. I found it ridiculously boring. I actually nodded off.

A half hour later the lawyer stepped into my cubicle and was amused to see my eyes were half closed. He took the time to sit with me and show me that contracts can actually be a game full of intrigue, manipulation, and suspense!

To understand a contract properly is to take in the entire story, all the intricate details of a deal. That's the story you're reading: a legal agreement between two entities. And if those entities are your own business and a major Hollywood studio—well, how much more exciting could it be?

Start learning how to read and understand contracts now. Visit the websites for the Screen Actors Guild, the Writers Guild, and the Directors Guild. All have a "Contract" section. Read them.

Never sign a contract if you haven't read it thoroughly yourself. Ever. It's your life and financial well-being at stake here. If you're feeling pressured by a producer or assistant director who wants you to quickly sign an agreement before you work, find a way to professionally distance yourself. Carefully read what you're signing. They'll wait. And they'll respect your attention to detail.

Usually your agent, manager, or lawyer will have seen the agreement before you do—but that is no excuse not to do your due diligence. I can recount many tales of agents making mistakes in contracts or missing small but crucial bits of information. (Hint: a decimal point can have cataclysmic impact.)

In particular, make certain you are clear about financial, exclusivity, ownership of image, and nudity clauses. There is no such thing as a stupid question about a contract, so don't be afraid to ask. Online research goes a long way, too.

Make sure you're clear about all the terms, even if it's a standard union contract. Producers can add "riders" to a contract that can jeopardize your well-being. In the end, if something goes wrong contractually, you bear sole responsibility.

Unions

Eventually you'll be a card-carrying member of the Screen Actors Guild–American Federation of Television and Radio Artists, also known as SAG-AFTRA.

Unions were created to protect you by regulating workplace conditions. They try to do a good job of it. They make certain your financial and physical well-being is taken care of on set. They provide health and retirement plans. And now that SAG and AFTRA are joined as one union, they're even more powerful.

An actor can be eligible for membership in the union in two ways. You can join with proof of SAG or AFTRA employment, or with proof of an affiliated performers' union.

At the beginning of your career, it can be difficult to become a member. The situation is a bit of a Catch-22: you can't get work in a SAG-AFTRA project if you aren't a member, and you can't be a member if you haven't worked in a SAG-AFTRA project!

The answer to the dilemma is getting "Taft-Hartley-ed" into the union. Taft-Hartley is the Labor Management Relations Act of 1947. It allows you to be hired into a SAG-AFTRA project even if you're not a member of the union, provided the producer affirms that you're an exceptional talent—essentially, the only person who can play that part.

Now all you have to do is find the production that believes you're that person. It happens every day in Hollywood. Many television commercials lead to the "Taft-Hartley-ing" of new members.

You can get your career started without being a union member. There are plenty of nonunion jobs in both commercials and television and film. Those jobs are not regulated, however, so you must be even more diligent to make certain you will be taken care of and not exploited in any way.

Visit the SAG-AFTRA website and follow the membership links to "Steps to Join" to get an in-depth look at the process of joining.

Actor's Equity Association is the union that represents actors working in theaters nationally. There are three different ways to become a member: working under an Equity contract at an Equity theater, through the Equity Membership Candidate Program, or through sister unions like SAG-AFTRA. Check union websites for updates or changes to the membership programs and protocols.

Once you're a member, bear in mind that the union is there for you. Make sure it's working for you. Check into the health and financial planning possibilities. Take advantage of the many powerful assists the union can provide. Go to the meetings, find out how the union works, perhaps even run to be a local board member. Get involved and let the union help you create a vibrant future as an actor.

Lawyers

Early in your career, you'll have little need for a personal entertainment lawyer. However, if you are without an agent or manager and you have to sign a legal document, it may be wise to hire someone. If you're financially challenged, remember that many law offices do pro bono (free) work for a small percentage of their clients. There are also cheap and easy online legal assists.

If you have a talent agent, you will be fairly well protected, as most agents handle the negotiation of contracts for their clients. This is not something talent managers are expected to do. In recent years, I've seen more and more actors hiring independent counsel to do their negotiating. One client had his quote doubled with his first lawyer negotiation. When I was a beginning writer without literary representation, I retained a good New York City lawyer to make my deals. It proved a wise investment.

Once you find yourself working steadily, it's almost imperative that you hire a law firm. The deals can be complex and have huge impact on your career arc, business and financial affairs, and life.

Agents

Talent agents procure auditions for you with casting directors. They typically take care of all communication between you and the company that hires you. They often handle the negotiations and contractual work as well.

At the start of your career, you may find it difficult to get signed by an agency. This is understandable, given that there are many small companies like yours who provide the same service. Agencies are inundated with requests for representation. They naturally protect themselves from actors who don't understand the business and don't respect professional boundaries. The doors are usually closed to new talent.

How to address this? First, you must work on the quality of your craft. Remember my equation for success. Quality always rises. Make the quality of your work world-class. And be ready to work at a moment's notice. You never know when the call will come for that audition or meeting.

Second, do blind submissions. Submit your headshot, resume, and links to your reel to agents in mass emails or mailings. Most agencies provide an email address to accept blind submissions. There are also services that will send online blind submissions to agents for a fee. My clients have had limited success with this approach.

Third, you must announce to the world that you are here. The best way to do that is to create an outstanding example of your work, either in a self-tape, short film, web series, or (as I did) by creating a play to showcase your talent. (Doing theater in Los Angeles is hard to recommend. This is a film and television town.) When the agents get word that you're a talented, creative artist, they'll want to work with you. You need to raise yourself above the crowd of many newcomers to find representation.

Fourth, there are companies that specialize in creating workshops and seminars where actors can be vetted by agents and industry professionals. Many are legitimate and helpful. However, there have been cases of financial abuse and a pay-for-play scandal in recent years with casting directors taking advantage of young actors. Tread carefully and do your own due diligence.

The best way to get in the door of a potential agency is through personal referrals. Networking is important, though you must handle this with discretion and tact. Do not cross boundaries or disrespect personal relationships that others have spent years building. It's best to wait for your network to get buzzing from your good work. People may then offer their assistance.

If they don't, it's your call as to when and how you make your request. But take good care—you can damage important relationships by being too self-promoting. The key to this type of referral is your work. Good work is delightful and infectious. Everyone wants to be part of it.

Networking with fellow actors won't usually solve the agent-finding dilemma. The folks you want to network with are producers, directors, writers, designers, crew members, and other industry professionals. And don't forget the friends and family connections you may have. Most people are more than willing to put in a good word for a talented, respectful, responsible person.

When you sign with an agency, you'll begin auditioning for all the casting directors in town. Naturally, you'll be eager to get out as often as you can. Believe me, your new agent wants that for you as well. Everyone wants you to make money! But different agents have different levels of power. Hollywood is built on personal reputations. A lower-level agency may simply not have the reputation to get you in for high-level work.

You may have to start at a lower level. That's fine. The important thing you must build with your representation is trust. You have to trust that they're doing their best to get you in the door. And they have to trust that you'll show up for your auditions in your best possible form.

Once you're auditioning, booking work, and making money, you'll no doubt experience periods of unemployment. This is natural. These periods can be challenging, but you must maintain perspective and a real understanding of what your agent is or is not doing on your behalf.

If your agency is unable to get you regular auditions, you need to sit down with them and discuss your options. Perhaps they're getting feedback from casting directors that you need to hear. Perhaps you need to make adjustments in your work. Perhaps they've lost their enthusiasm for you. Perhaps you need to create a new project to reinvigorate everyone. You're the boss of your company, and you must find ways to motivate your staff to work hard for you.

If they still can't get you in the door, consider finding new representation. Their job is to procure you auditions. If they aren't doing their job, be a professional businessperson and fire them. It isn't easy, but there's nothing sadder than watching talented clients tread water for extensive periods waiting for their reps to get them auditions.

One of my clients was signed by one of the biggest agencies in the world. It was exciting at first, but beneath the surface, he sensed the tension in the agency. The longer he stayed, the more he felt the sexism, racism, and cutthroat competition. He found that stress toxic. I will forever be proud of him for firing that agency and moving to another one—where he's happily stayed for many years.

Managers

The difference between managers and agents is a bit blurry. In early Hollywood, only talent agencies represented actors. Then managers started to work on their behalf, usually in a mentoring, advisory role. Managers help build their clients' foundations by finding acting coaches, headshot photographers, publicists, and so on. Many managers handle celebrity endorsement deals and other venues of income for their clients that agents don't. Over time, the manager has become someone who gets auditions for talent as well.

Agents are licensed by the state, which gives them the legal right to solicit auditions for you. That license also allows them to negotiate your contracts. Managers, not being licensed, generally let the agent do that work. Legally, managers are not supposed to book auditions, but today they often do.

Sometimes an actor will have both a manager and an agent, sometimes just one or the other. The industry is so competitive that I recommend you have both.

By law, agents are not allowed to take more than 10 percent of the gross income of the contract. Most managers follow suit and take 10 percent, although some now take 15 percent. Some managers work on a sliding scale. You will have to negotiate the terms of your agreement with them.

Agents can have up to 150 clients. Managers tend to have no more than fifty. This gives them the time to pay more attention to each client's needs and development. In my experience, managers tend to be better suited for the emotional support an artist needs, whereas the agent provides the business/legal support.

Managers tend to take commission on all your entertainment industry earnings, so be warned. Agents take only their fee for the work that they get for you.

To find a manager, take the same four steps as you would to find an agent: make your work outstanding, create new work that shows you off, do blind submissions, and use your connections.

You're the Boss

If you pay people, they work for you. Some of those people don't look at it that way, but if you hire people, they're your staff. Treat them with dignity and respect but remember, you're the boss.

Meetings

Most actors like to be social and enjoy entertaining others. Why, then, do so many actors find business meetings difficult? For one thing, you may feel disempowered in a business setting by the status of the people involved. In many meetings, you won't hold the cards.

You may be comfortable in front of a camera, but here you aren't playing a character. You have no solid script. This is not a performance. Don't pretend to be more together, connected, or successful than you truly are.

Simple etiquette comes first. Be on time, be prepared, be polite, turn off your phone, and do more listening than speaking. Take the measure of the people around you. (You can bet they're assessing you.) This is another place where your bullshit meter comes in handy. There are people who are naturally smooth and charming. And then there are people who are too smooth, too charming.

It is important to know what you want from a meeting. What do you hope to see advanced, decided, resolved, or agreed upon? Don't just float through a meeting if it's not moving in the direction you want to go. A bad meeting is one you leave asking yourself, "What the hell was that all about?" A good meeting is one you leave feeling that you've taken a concrete step forward.

12
Working

Heatless in Bulgaria

I once shot a TV movie in Sofia, Bulgaria. It was November, and deep winter had already set in. Our film took place in summer, so our costumes were made of the thinnest materials. Now, I grew up in western Canada, so I understand cold. This wasn't just cold. This was fucking freezing.

The first day of the shoot, I was chilled to the bone. It was so cold and miserable that I seriously, for the first time in my career, considered quitting a project. I just couldn't see how I was going to survive.

That evening, soaking in a hot tub in my hotel room, trying to warm my bones back to room temperature, I knew I had to find a way to use the cold. Make everything make you better.

Freezing in Bulgaria with Eric Roberts, ice cold as the blood in our characters' veins.

I realized that my character was a cold-hearted sonofabitch. His blood ran cold. He was capable of extreme violence. I decided that the temperature outside would be my temperature inside.

The next day on set I embraced the weather to inform my character. I'm not saying I didn't still have the occasional shiver, but at least I didn't quit the film!

Farty

A client of mine was once on a set with a well-known and gifted actor. On the first day of shooting, The Star's way of staying loose was to make a joke just before the camera rolled. He would fart, or say something silly, anything to make people laugh. It was The Star's way of dealing with the pressure of performance, his way of processing. It was part of his launch primer.

My client was playing the bad guy. To do that, he had to keep himself in a serious, earnest place. His character's world was grave and dark, not humorous and farty. My client is a lovely guy and tried to get along with The Star. But the jokes threw him off. They took him out of his focus. He felt his work suffering.

Clearly, their approaches to their work collided. My client called me that evening, unsure what to do. He didn't want to be a bore and stop the others from laughing. But he also didn't want to have his work diminished. And he certainly didn't want to build a negative relationship with The Star.

I had to help my client make this work to his advantage. How could he learn from this situation and create a better reality for himself on set? We opened up the script and my client's workbook.

It didn't take long to realize that, in the character history my client had created, the character had been bullied. People had been laughing at him and playing jokes on him his whole life. That's why his world was so dark and why he did the evil things he did. Aha! We had the answer!

The following day on set, my client simply laughed at the fart jokes and then told himself that his character had just been made fun of and laughed at by all the people around him. And bam! It put him right into the character. It worked for him! It helped his character pop to life every take!

Take the Character Out into Public

A very straight/masculine/macho ex-college football player client of mine surprised us all one day when he booked the role of a drag queen named "Sally" in a major motion picture shooting in the Caribbean. (Names in this story have definitely been changed to protect the innocent!)

After much laughter and a month of getting into Sally's history, motivations, and secrets, we finally got down to the wire. My client was due to fly out to play the part and still hadn't taken Sally out in public. I was adamant that he do this to solidify his self-confidence in playing a drag queen. The last place I wanted him existing publicly as Sally for the first time would be on the set. That was a recipe for certain disaster.

But my client had a hard time going out in drag in Los Angeles. He felt that for certain he would be recognized and TMZ'ed to death. As much as I pushed him to do the deed and let Sally out in LA, he simply couldn't do it.

I couldn't force him to do this and let him know how disappointed and worried I was by his lack of bravery. He promised me that he would take Sally for a spin in the tropics. "Talk to the hand, honey."

I was happily surprised the day after his flight when he called to tell me he had indeed dolled up in his hotel room and bravely stepped into the hallway. He said that the moment his hotel room door opened, he felt the character of

Sally deeply inside him for the first time. He walked the long hallway to the elevator in his heels, feeling every inch the woman he was hired to be.

To his surprise, when the elevator door opened, it revealed a US Marine in complete formal dress uniform. My client smiled and entered the elevator and was surprised to hear these words come out of his own mouth: "Well, look at the two of us! Both in formal dress!"

Even better, now full of bravado, when he stepped into a cab at the hotel's front door, a passing teenager bullied him by saying, "Hey lady, are you gay?"—to which my wide-shouldered client spiced back, "I'm very happy, thank you very much."

Sally was alive!

Unlocking Emotion

Years ago, I was directing a young actor in a big scene for a short film. It was a high-stakes moment for the character and therefore a big emotional moment for this actor.

He was pushing himself hard. Unfortunately, he'd made the mistake of making an appointment. He wanted to cry, basically. He wanted to be a good actor and break down crying. But he couldn't get there because he was so concerned about crying. His emotional tool wasn't strong enough. The more he tried to get upset and cry, the more locked up he became. The more locked up he became, the more his frustration grew. He worked himself into a state of tremendous anger and frustration.

We did a few takes. He got more and more worked up, brutally chastising himself for his lack of capacity to cry. It wasn't helping. I quietly pulled him aside and said to him, "All right, let's stop for a moment. You know this horribly intense feeling that you have right now in your tummy?"

"Yeah."

"You feel like you're a really bad actor."

"Yes."

"You feel like a failure, like you're never going to have a career as an actor."

"Yes, fuck, Craig!"

"Well, does that make you sad?"

"Yeah."

"Use that terrible feeling. Just let it out. Use that sad."

He took a deep breath and relaxed and boom! Tears! Beautiful! We turned the camera on and got it. It was a breakthrough in his emotional availability. He finally was able to allow himself to be truly vulnerable.

Be on Time!

This may seem obvious but being punctual is the most important thing you can do in this industry. There's an old adage in Hollywood that being on time is late. Being fifteen minutes early is being on time.

A client of mine was in second position for a major television job as a recurring character on an HBO show. To her disappointment, they chose another young woman to play the part. Shockingly, that actor was late to work for the first two days in a row. The morning of the second day, the executive producer called my client and asked her if she could come into work. She could. They fired the first actress on the spot, and my client replaced her in the recurring role on the show. It ran for three years.

Be on time.

Know Who the Players Are

There are many people who work on a television show or movie. You don't have to know all of the people in all of the positions, but you absolutely have to know who the people in power are. These include the showrunner (the lead producer and often the creator of the television show), the producers, the director, and their first and second assistants. Sometimes, women in particular will have meetings with costume, hair, and makeup folks before the first day.

To be clear: On a film set, the director is the boss. On a television set, the boss is the showrunner. (Beware of those producers with deep pockets and shallow taste who think they are the boss—they aren't.)

How you interact with these people is important. They have hired you to do a job and for the most part will trust that you can do that job and leave you to it. However, from time to time they will give you notes on your performance. Handling those notes with grace and dignity is essential and should be part of your training. The difficulty arises when you disagree with a note. The ability to discuss your differences artfully with these people is very important. You will often have done deeper and more specific homework on the character than they ever would have the time for. That's OK, that's your job. Sharing with them your discoveries may guide them in their interpretation of the character so that you can come to a mutually agreed-upon point of view.

Basing your performance on your audition is basic protocol. We do not make wildly different choices after we have booked the role without specific discussions with the boss. Hopefully this work is done in meetings, phone calls, or even the rare rehearsal with the boss before you are on the set. If you do not get that time and attention, bring what you brought to the audition.

Sadly, one of my young actors didn't understand who everyone was on the set of his first costarring role. After he'd been wrapped for the day, he called me to report his experience. Everything had gone well "except for a producer who kept giving me notes." I asked who that producer was and my client told me the name of the showrunner. He had spent the day ignoring the acting notes from the showrunner because he thought the director was the only person who could give him notes. This disaster meant that they had no choice in the final edit but to cut much of his character because he simply didn't listen to the right person.

It is also important to know the first assistant director (AD). They are often the loud and bossy person who physically runs the set. They are the shepherd who gets the flock in place, quiet, and ready to shoot. The second AD helps them by being aware of the whereabouts of every sheep on the set. These folks are your friends. They can make your set life luxuriously comfortable or misanthropically miserable. Best to be on their good side. Inform them of your whereabouts and LISTEN to them when they speak to you.

Dumb and Dumber

I've had several clients book jobs on television shows where, when they show up on set, they're told to not do the "acting" they did in the audition but to just "say the lines."

This threw many of them off their game for a moment. It doesn't make sense to people with artistic integrity. But some television channels cater to a particular audience, and the powers that be have decided that "good" acting is no acting. Somehow, in a producer world of numbers and approval ratings, this makes sense.

My advice was to follow the direction, but to keep all the work they did in getting the part and make it their "secret" in the scene. And it worked. In watching the finished product, my clients weren't embarrassed by acting that was empty—it was just subtle!

The twist here is that my clients had to be very good to book the roles. All of them did a lot of homework, worked hard with me before the audition, then went in and nailed it. Casting directors and producers are using the best actors they can, but then dumbing down the work. It's a bizarre phenomenon, but it happens. Be ready for anything.

Paparazzi

A client recently shot a film in Manhattan. His costar was a big name, which meant that a gaggle of paparazzi followed them from location to location. My client was having trouble ignoring them, and the distraction was interfering with his ability to do his work. He called me in a bit of a panic.

"I can't concentrate. I can't focus. I hate having still cameras on set here."

"How can we turn this around, so they help you concentrate and focus?"

"I don't know," he said. "Every time I see a still photographer in my eye line, I become self-conscious. And these bastards are everywhere."

"First, your in-the-moment muscle is weak. You have to make it stronger. Focus. And second, you're making this all about you. It should be about the character."

"So, how would the paparazzi affect my character?"

"You're playing a musician, right? At some level, don't musicians want attention? Don't they want to be looked at?"

Two days later, he called and said, "I was much better today. It's really helping. My focus is better. And my character, when he's working, does want to be looked at and admired. I'm letting the paparazzi feed that deep psychological need."

You're a Tool

Imagine being a director. You're standing in the center of a large circle of talent. All around you are departments full of tools available to help you tell your story. You have the writer/writer's room, production designers, editors, sound team, camera department, costumes, makeup, the producers, and, finally, the actors. In each of the departments, there are at least five to ten people.

As an actor, you're just one of the tools. This is not to insult you, but to inspire you. Be the best actor you can be so that you can help the director tell his story.

J. K. Simmons gave a wonderful acceptance speech when he won the Screen Actors Guild award for his best supporting actor performance in Damien Chazelle's *Whiplash*. He said, "We are all supporting actors, we are all supporting the story, and if one of us is false, plays a false note, the audience loses its ability to give us their willing suspension of disbelief, and we have to work harder to earn their trust again."

You Are on Mic

Never forget that you have a personal microphone on you. Usually it's a lavalier, tucked into the collar or neckline of your shirt. Remember what Thumper the rabbit said to Bambi in the classic Disney film? "If you can't say

On location, Fort Rucker, Alabama, 1996. Remember—you're on mic.

anything nice, don't say anything at all." This is wonderful on-set advice. If you have something to say that's not nice, turn off your mic!

I speak from experience. I took part in an unfortunate conversation that was recorded. I was speaking with another actor about how bad we thought the director was. I was lingually flamboyant, shall we say. That director won't speak to me to this day.

So remember: turn off your mic.

Eating in Costume

Don't do it! Always remember that you are dressed in a garment that is precious. It is easy to forget when you are hangry and attempt to slam some much-needed but potentially messy sustenance. Don't disrespect your colleagues in the costume department by slopping food or beverages onto their hard work.

Eating in a Scene

When you are required to eat in a scene, you must take great care to be specific and proactively defensive.

You must be able to repeat your performance for the editors to cut the scene using many different angles and takes. You must know exactly when you lift that fork or bread roll, when you put it in your mouth, and when you place it back on the plate. And you must do your best to repeat the action on every take.

Also, as a general rule, don't truly eat the food. You can do all kinds of activities without actually eating. You can cut the meat, butter the bread, or pass the bowl.

Be aware of noise you make with your cutlery. Sound editors will be grateful.

I also advise my clients to be very proactive in making certain that their utensils, plates, and glassware have all been properly sanitized. I've been known to wash my own props prior to using them in a scene.

Film and television sets are not held up to any kind of food handling safety standards or health codes. You have every right to ask questions concerning the objects you are being requested to ingest. Be careful.

A well-known television actress impressed me once when she refused to eat the shrimp the network had provided for a party scene. She first grilled the props crew on the date of purchase, expiration date, and refrigeration details, then she agreed to put the shrimp in her mouth but would not swallow it. She was not being a difficult actress. She was taking care of her health.

Drinking in a Scene

A similar type of discipline is required when drinking in a scene.

Again, you must repeat the action on the same line of dialogue for each take. If you don't, the editors will have a very difficult time cutting your scene. You do not want to have those folks frustrated with you.

Again, it is more than appropriate for you to check the cleanliness and/ or the source of the beverage you will be drinking. A beloved actor friend of mine had twenty-two years of sobriety under his belt when the props people accidentally put real beer in his beer bottle in a bar scene. He asked twice if it was fake beer. They insisted it was. Until it wasn't.

One of my clients on a low-budget SAG film took a swig of his beer in the first take of a scene and got a dirty cigarette filter in his mouth. The props folks hadn't cleaned the bottles. Horror stories like this happen all the time.

Smoking

Speaking of cigarettes, you absolutely need to be aware of when you take a drag off a cigarette in a scene. Smoking actually has three steps. One is the physical lifting of the hand to the face; two is the pulling in of the smoke into your lungs; three is the expelling of smoke. All three of these can make editors crazy if you are changing your behavior on every take.

Also, if you are not a smoker, you have every right to request herbal cigarettes—or to have a rider on your contract that specifically states you will not smoke on any job.

The Legalese of These

In general, your representation team should be aware of what you will be requested to do on a set—so any activity from stunts to eating and smoking should be handled in your contracts. Make certain your team is aware of your concerns, allergies, and any stipulations they may need to make production aware of.

Make certain your boundaries are clearly stated in your contract!

Hitting Marks

In order for the actor to be in focus for the camera, the camera crew place taped "marks" on the floor to guide the actor into place. This is called "hitting your mark." We do this in stage plays as well.

Proficiency in this skill is essential. Luckily, it is something you can easily practice in your home or hotel room when shooting on location. When working on a scene, you can create your own marks and practice hitting them. I recommend you practice prior to arriving on set. This can greatly calm nerves associated with blocking and camera elements you won't know until the day.

This is a basic acting skill set, but it is essential to your work, particularly when there is intricate choreography between yourself and a moving Steadicam operator.

I love watching old movie actors doing this. One in particular, Spencer Tracy, was a genius at it. Very often, he made looking at his mark part of the scene. He would look at the mark intensely as if he was processing his thoughts by looking down. Then he'd land on his mark and keep his head down in thought before finally coming back to the eyes of the other actors.

Remember, the audience has no idea what we see through our eyes from our perspective looking toward the camera and crew.

Sex Scenes and Nudity

As titillating or fun as these scenes may sound, in reality they are far from either. Very often, they are simply boring and uncomfortable for everyone.

You can improve the ambience by always being respectfully professional and polite.

The standard rule for kissing is that open mouths are fine but no tongues. It's always a good idea to carry a breath freshener and share it with your fellow performer liberally.

The rules for body contact are that you must work with your director and fellow performer closely and get approval for all movements and/or touching. Then only do that approved choreography or action with no improvising. Many sets now employ an intimacy coordinator to ensure these scenes are handled appropriately.

Make certain your representation knows and respects your boundaries regarding nudity. Double-check these clauses in your contract.

Remember, these scenes are simulated. This is not reality. Act accordingly and respectfully.

When You Are a Lead, You Are a Leader

The lead actor on a set is much like the quarterback of a football team. You are a leader. And your leadership skills should be taken seriously. Often, the behavior and attitude of the actor who is number one on the call sheet sets the tone for the entire set. I instruct my clients who book leading roles to think of themselves as the lighthouse in the storm. Yes, your job is to be the character, but that doesn't stop you from being polite and kind to the many people who are working hard to make you look good.

Having a sense of humor is important and can often save a difficult moment from getting enflamed. But be careful not to joke too much.

This recently happened on a popular studio comedy shoot. On the morning of the first day, the actors were having so much fun that they couldn't finish the takes without cracking up. The crew had a jolly time too with all of the hysterical ad-libs and laughter. By lunchtime, they realized they were behind schedule. The afternoon wasn't much better for scheduling, but they were having a lovely time laughing, so who cared?

That evening, the lead actor received a call in his hotel room from the president of the studio. The president politely asked, "How was your day?" The actor replied that it had "been a lot of fun, thanks, how was yours?" The president replied, "Not so great. You see, I have a movie that is costing me one million dollars a day to produce and my actors joked away half the day and cost me $500,000." The actor stayed silent, so the president continued. "Waste more of my money and I will fire your ass. I do not care how famous or funny you are."

Fame

In the words of the talented writer Michael Albanese, "We are not made to bear the weight of idolatry."

These are words of earned wisdom. Young actors are often excited by the idea of fame. They believe it comes as part of the deal with fortune. This is dangerous. In my humble interactions with fame, it is more often a considerable blight on a life and far from fun or sexy. It is devoid of almost any value of any kind.

Unfortunately, the rush of early fame is intoxicating, and unless you are very grounded, it can swallow you whole. This is not a pleasant journey. When you are swallowed whole, you are eventually excreted as shit. I know this image is graphic, but it's true! And it's a very difficult day/month/year or two to say the least.

Being number one on a call sheet is a big deal. And you are treated as royalty. Not because you ARE royalty, but because you are the FACE of the project. It's difficult to be in that position. It takes a lot of focus, discipline, and hard work to be a successful leading actor.

The off-set life of a lead actor can also be perilous. One can get used to assistants and sycophants offering up all kinds of favors. Never waiting in line, always walked to the front. Having drivers, assistants, makeup artists, and hair people flitting about you answering your every whim—it can become addictive.

Unfortunately, when you get home to your partner and kids, they don't see you as the star. You are the parent. The partner. Not number one on the call sheet. This can be a difficult reckoning for the entire household.

While I'm on the subject of children: Please do not have kids unless you understand that they are not accessories. This mistake isn't exclusively made in show business, but it can be prevalent here.

The only good thing I've found about fame is that it can be helpful when trying to raise philanthropic goals. That's about the only time I've seen it do any good.

With Alyssa Sutherland at the Elton John AIDS Foundation Academy Award Party, 2016.

Playback and Dailies

On some sets, you are given the opportunity to take a look at the playback of a take you have just done. This is more common on film sets than television sets. On film locations, there are often viewings of the "dailies" or what you shot that day or the day before.

Be careful about your decision to watch or not watch your work. You are the only one who knows how watching yourself affects you. Absolutely do not watch if you know you are going to go into some horrible shame spiral about your nose or hair or weight. When you are shooting is not the time for acting class. If you watch yourself, do not fall into a self-judgment pit of despair; use the opportunity to create the best performance you can and that is all.

Complaining Club

Confusing sarcasm with sophistication is a common mistake. This is a problem that usually starts in high school or college. This ideology usually shows up on sets in the form of complaining. All you need is two complainers to form a club and negativity is off to the races.

Be smart and have nothing to do with the complaining club. Seriously, just walk away if someone starts complaining. Or say nothing at all. Just because they mouth off, that doesn't mean you have to agree or say anything. The best move is to get away from them or say nothing at all.

A client booked a recurring role on an ABC/Freeform television show for young people. He was one of a group of seven recurring actors. He was terrifically excited, and the night before his first day, we chatted briefly about his prep and expectations. I reminded him that there would more than likely be some kind of complaining club in his recurring gang and that he should not engage.

The following evening, he called as he drove home from the set. He was excited to tell me that indeed there was a group of young actors who did nothing but complain. At lunch, he moved to another table so he wouldn't be associated with them and their bad behavior. He was joined by several other recurring actors who didn't want to complain but instead discussed basketball and current movies.

None of us was surprised to learn at the end of the first week that three of the actors in the complaining club had been let go.

True sophistication means you handle yourself with grace and dignity at all times.

Stuck in the Nineties

An actor I know is famous from a television show he starred in during the 1990s. He was a major star for the show's ten-year run. Unfortunately, that show typecast him as the character, and he's had little acting work since. People simply cannot see him as any other character. Ironically, his great success was also the seed of his demise as an actor.

For ten years, he was famous and celebrated. He was even invited to the White House. Today, he's instantly recognized when he travels. People are excited to meet him, and he remains kind, charming, and proud of his famous work. Imagine how trying it is to constantly be called the name of a character you haven't played in more than twenty years.

He was wise with his money and invested in a new kind of technology connected to what was then called "the World Wide Web." He never fails to be grateful for his acting success but even more for the wisdom to invest wisely. That investment has funded the rest of his life.

A Pandemic Success Story

After the heart-crushing spring of 2020, when COVID-19 changed all our lives, the film and television industry slowly returned to work that fall. Despite heavy hearts, it was a relief to return to the trenches and an adjusted new reality.

A young client, just getting his start in the industry, jubilantly informed me that he had booked a costar role on a well-known series on a high-end cable television channel. Although the virus was still rampant, he celebrated with a very small group of his family bubble the weekend before the shoot dates.

Unbeknownst to him, one of the bubble members was an asymptomatic carrier of the virus. When my client reported to set several days later, he was shocked to learn that he had tested positive for the virus.

Casting immediately sent him home and replaced him with another actor within hours.

This would normally be a difficult blow to an actor. Not only was he let go from a great career-starting role; he was now sick with a deadly disease.

Out of tremendous concern, I maintained frequent interaction with him to confirm his well-being, both physically and mentally.

Remarkably, I didn't have to be concerned about either. Yes, he was physically ill for a difficult week. But what was surprisingly beautiful was his resilience. He was downright positive about the experience, never accepting my concern that he would, could, or should be upset. He saw absolutely nothing but positives. To him, simply booking the role had proven that he could book work at the highest level. Losing the job was not about his integrity or his artistry, it was about a highly contagious disease. Period.

Talk about making everything make you better! I am so proud of this young man. He stepped up beyond my expectation of champion, and I look forward to celebrating his many successes to come.

The Unkindest Cut

In August 2005, I got a call informing me that my work in the Sony Pictures Classics movie *Capote* had been cut from the final edit. I'd been cast about a year earlier and filmed my scenes—all with Philip Seymour Hoffman—in Winnipeg, Manitoba, in November 2004 and New York in the spring of 2005. I'd had plenty of time to tell pretty much every person I knew that I was in a movie with one of the greatest actors of my generation.

My friend, the late David Rakoff and I were cast as New York literati pals of Truman Capote, but our scenes were cut to shave precious minutes off the final running time. About a month after that phone call, *Capote* opened the New York Film Festival. I was a bundle of ego, devastation, and knocked-flat disappointment. And yet, there I was on the red carpet with a dear friend on my arm.

The screening was a huge hit. Phil, along with screenwriter Dan Futterman and actor Catherine Keener (who portrayed Harper Lee), received roaring applause onstage after the screening. It was a beautiful moment for all of us. Danny said some profoundly kind words from the stage, thanking me for my help on his screenplay. At the post screening party, Philip, Catherine, and Danny were all lovely and a good time was had by all.

God bless my dear friend who, inspired by several glasses of champagne, sensed a quiet disappointment from me in the limo on the way home. "You have to listen to me, honey. You were an important part of the making of a good film. Who cares if you were chopped? All the greats have stories of being cut from films! You have a choice right here and now. You can choose to be a victim and ride the misery train, or you can be proud of your contribution and stand up tall and celebrate your part of helping to make this good film."

It was a great lesson. Some things you can control and some you can't. Scenes get rewritten. Directors get fired. Whole films are made but never released. You have the power to choose the response that lifts you.

With Danny Futterman the weekend he got the idea for his screenplay of *Capote*. Barnegat Light, Long Beach Island, New Jersey, 1998.

13

Business Savvy

During my forty years in this business, I've seen many people succeed as actors, writers, directors, and producers. There's no grand mystery. It's not some cosmic joke forcing you to struggle. It's an industry, and the artists who succeed are the ones who recognize this and embrace it. If you fear it, if you build it into a monster, you'll be doing yourself a disservice. You're on a potential life journey that is rewarding beyond words.

I've seen many film scripts come to life as fully produced movies. I've seen five scripts go from the page in front of me to the Academy Awards! You can do this. I've seen many different types of people achieve their goals in the film industry. Why not you?

The Inside

An issue of *Film Comment* magazine carries an interview with director James L. Brooks. He's considered one of the top directors in Hollywood. He was a writer on classic television hits *The Mary Tyler Moore Show* and *Taxi*; he directed many Academy Award–winning films, including *Terms of Endearment* and *As Good as It Gets*. You may recognize his name as the executive producer of *The Simpsons*.

Brooks was quoted as follows: "I always think of myself as on the outside looking in. And I have all these fantasies about the inside—in there, people are having a good time, all the time. That's true. Isn't it?"

The interviewer said, "You see yourself as an outsider? You're regarded as a powerful Hollywood insider."

Brooks replied, "Well, that's just not true."

That's about when I tossed the magazine on to the floor. I mean, come on! The man has Jack Nicholson in every movie he's done! And as I sat and stewed, a little light went off in my head. Could it be that, as Gertrude Stein said of Oakland, there is no there there?

In his home on the bank of the Hudson River, Al Pacino insisted to me that he wasn't on the "inside"—that it had been fifteen years since he'd won the Oscar and he now did his work happily outside the mainstream.

I recall a television interview with Tom Hanks in which he also said he wasn't a Hollywood insider, that it had been many years since his back-to-back wins for best actor.

A client who's worked for Steven Spielberg told me that Spielberg feels the same way—it's been more than ten years since he won the Oscar.

So, wait a second. If James L. Brooks, Al Pacino, Tom Hanks, and Steven Spielberg aren't insiders, who is?

I've never met an actor who isn't worried about future work. I've never met a director who hasn't feared his project won't be greenlit. I've never met a producer who isn't looking over their shoulder, praying the choices they've made will pay off. There's not a writer who isn't churning with doubt. Not a casting director, not a set designer, not a prop person, not a single soul in this industry really feels secure. Wouldn't being on "the inside" make you secure?

Guess what? There's no fabled place where everyone is happy and cool and rich and assured of endless contracts under the setting sun off Malibu. There's no Hollywood Hills party where the laughter rains down upon the selected few who feel safe in this ever-shifting landscape. There is no "inside."

Therefore, there's no reason to feel bad because you aren't there. If you're struggling (and who isn't? I hear it every day, even from my movie star clients), you're just compounding your frustration if you worry about not being on the inside. It's a waste of time.

If there's no "inside" in the industry, the only real inside is this. You reading this. The right now. The moment by moment. Every second of every minute of your day. The energy you put into your art. The actions you take to move your business forward. The classes, the conversations, the care, the attention to the life you lead, the love you share. This is it. Your life is the only inside that matters.

So if this is it, make it good. Celebrate it. Enjoy it. Work hard. Then relax. Be happy. You're rich in the most important way. The sun sets off Malibu every day, for everyone.

Quit Judging People

One afternoon in the early 2000s, I'd just left my apartment in the West Village of Manhattan when I ran into an old friend. We'd both worked at the same bar. Jeff, in my mind, was a smart, cute, funny, up-and-coming writer. During our chat, he said he was working on a new musical that used puppets. He said it was a kind of fun musical—an adult version of the children's television show Sesame Street.

I tried not to roll my eyes. Puppets? Come on, seriously? In my naive snobbery, I changed the subject, probably to something far more interesting (like my still-unpublished novel). As I walked away, I remember thinking, "Good luck with the puppets!"

I couldn't have been more wrong. Two years later, Jeff Whitty won the Tony award for Best Book of a Musical for the brilliantly funny musical *Avenue Q*.

Don't judge others. You never know what kooky idea might become the next mother lode of a hit.

Take Inspiration

Your fellow artists provide inspiration you can put directly into your own work. Dive into the visual arts: painting, drawing, sculpture, photography, ceramics, pottery. Revel in the performing arts: dance, singing, music. Find your muse in the applied arts: fashion, architecture, interior design, landscape architecture, woodcraft, jewelry design. Disappear into literature: novels, poetry, plays, short stories. Celebrate your life by baking, winemaking, cooking, chocolatiering!

And of course, take inspiration from your fellow actors and the films, television shows, and stage plays they work in. Creativity and artistry take many forms. Channel the stimulation and energy they provide into your own work.

Don't Be a Fan on Set

You must not let your adoration for a fellow actor interfere with your job. If you've been hired to work with an actor, you've been put on par with them. Engaging in idol worship is embarrassing and boring. It also gets in the way of the work.

An actress worked with a Major Film Star on the set of a dramatic film. She was excited to work with him and made a big thing of it.

The Major Film Star said to her in front of the crew, "It's important to you that I like you, isn't it?"

The actress said, "Yes."

"It shouldn't be," said the Major Film Star.

Embarrassed, the actress went into a silent funk for the rest of the day.

That evening, as they were wrapping up, there was a knock at her trailer. The Major Film Star walked in and hugged her and said, "There. Now let's be equals, friends, and good actors and kill this bitch."

The Green-Eyed Monster

Jealousy doesn't help. At all. Let it go. Be happy that your friends (or enemies) are succeeding. If they can do it, so can you. Don't waste your precious energy.

Don't Be a Baby

Every actor has difficult days. It can be difficult at times not to stomp and pout and want the world to treat you with the respect you self-righteously know you deserve.

You do deserve it! But you can't allow yourself to be unprofessional. Buck up, bite your lip, and follow through, fulfilling the commitment you made to the project.

I've received many cranky phone calls from actors in distress. One client had so much work done on her hair that it infuriated the leading lady of the film, who insisted the hair crew pay her more attention. Ultimately, the leading lady had the entire hair crew fired two weeks before Christmas.

One of my clients was on set with fellow actors who convinced the director/writer to give them most of my actor's lines.

One of my New York actors flew out to Los Angeles to audition for a film and was called "babe" and "buddy" by the casting director. The New York actor saw this as "Hollywood." It made him crazy enough that he mimicked the casting director to his face, sarcastically calling him "buddy" and "babe." He won't be called back to that office soon.

A female client was cast opposite a male model. He was so green they had to give him dozens of takes to get decent work. This ate up so much of the shooting schedule that my actress often got only a single take.

I have many such stories. The point is this: It's never going to be perfect. You must be ready for the arrows that come your way. You must not be a baby. Sometimes it's just a job. Do your best and move on.

Don't Let Your Ego Fuck Things Up

This is a good life lesson in general. But in our world of performing, it is essential to keeping your wits about you and succeeding.

The ego is a deceptive part of the human psyche. It can slice in with a killer comment out of the dark and damage you more harshly than any enemy. It can creep up quietly and surprise you at your most vulnerable moments. For me, the true answer to dealing with it is in meditation. Meditation has helped me tremendously in keeping it well identified and for the most part at a distance.

The confusing thing here is that a healthy ego is necessary to survive the constant onslaught of judgment and rejection we suffer in this industry.

When it comes to performance, it is essential to understand and be practiced (by being in class) in the way your personal ego helps and hurts you.

In general, when an actor serves their ego, the body shuts down out of fear and a wooden, uptight, and/or angst-ridden performance follows.

When an actor serves the character and makes the scene about the other characters, the body relaxes and opens up. This predicates a truly open, free, and fun performance.

Listening

I've had clients work with some of the biggest names in the industry, and it's always disappointing to learn that a particular actor or actress doesn't listen.

You would be horrified to hear how many big-name actors don't listen and often come in on the wrong cue or simply barge ahead with their lines, whether it makes true sense to the scene or not.

Don't be that actor. Hear me?

The Secret to a Happy Life as an Actor

You have to marry the love of the art form to the doing of the art form. Do not marry the love to results. Love doing it and you will always have positive results. Love results and you will always have negative doings.

Be Smart

Wisdom comes with experience. Yes, you can read this book and perhaps feel a little wiser, but it's only when you put lessons learned into action that you really take on fundamental truths.

So get active. Create the project that will make your next step happen. Whether writing a screenplay or producing a web series or taking your manager out for lunch, do things that will push you toward the next level of your work.

And don't be afraid of failure. The adage that you learn more from failure than success is true. The more you do, the more you learn. The more you learn, the more you know. And the more you know, the more likely you are to succeed.

Wisdom truly does come through experience, so get out there and gain all the experience, of all sorts, that you can.

Burden or Opportunity?

Being an artist and creating your small business in Hollywood is not a burden. It's a universe of potential. And the way you see your universe is the way it will be revealed to you. It's your choice. You're the boss. Everything you think and do has a role in determining how your life will play out.

Actors and Athletes

Like athletes, actors must work continuously to improve their skill set. Both actors and athletes need discipline. Training. Focus. Sacrifice. Their in-the-moment muscle. The ability to perform under pressure. Openness to criticism.

Kobe Bryant, the beloved Los Angeles Lakers star, would start practicing three to four hours before anyone else. He'd taken eight hundred shots before the rest of the team arrived. J. J. Watt of the NFL Houston Texans is famous for staying later than his teammates. He works deep into the night perfecting and honing his abilities. In the off-season, he flips thousand-pound tires. No wonder he has a forty-one-inch vertical leap.

Where do you think the genius and in-the-moment focus of tennis great Rafael Nadal comes from? Or the success of the swimmer with the most Olympic medals in history, Michael Phelps? He was famous for spending hours longer in the pool than his competitors. If you want to be a great athlete, you must pay the price. The same goes for actors.

Those who go deepest win.

Secondary Income

Most actors need a secondary income. Make it make you better. If you work in a restaurant or bar, find positives in your experience. It's simply a matter of having the right frame of mind. You can get angry and upset at the crazy lady at table sixteen, or you can watch her behavior carefully, take note of it, and use it in something that you're creating. Put it in your journal of real-life behavior!

If you work in an office, study your bosses to learn the dos and don'ts of running a company, handling staff, managing a crisis. Corporate America offers business lessons, both positive and negative, that you can apply to your own small business. Look and learn from your support job. For an actor, it's a free education.

Have you considered starting your own company? I have a client with a T-shirt company; another runs a website-design company; another makes car-seat protectors for dog owners; another owns the route to deliver potato chips to all the markets in West Los Angeles. Find a way to create a secondary small business that will pay for your life while you create your primary small business—your acting career.

All these people run their own small companies. These are businesses that provide an income and are easy to leave (with trained staff in place) if they have an audition or shoot.

And don't ignore your skill set. I have a client who happily makes a very good second income doing voice-over commercial work and recording audiobooks. Not only is she using her acting skill set daily; she is also adding points to her SAG medical insurance and retirement savings. Plus, she works from her home recording studio in her pajamas.

The Zen Zone

When you've done all your homework and dug as deep as you can; when you bring your true human vulnerability and live truthfully as the character; when you're fully connecting with the eyes of the other characters, you sometimes achieve a kind of Zen. It's the reward for all your hard work.

It's a delicious place to be. You feel as if you are the character. You believe the other actors are the other characters. You're free and flying and having just about the most fun possible on this planet. Those who have experienced this Zen zone know it to be the greatest feeling. One of my goals in sharing the information in this book is to help you achieve this intense and exalted experience.

Capote

In *Capote*, I was cast in the role of Christopher Isherwood. He's one of my favorite novelists, so it was a particular pleasure to portray him. I did my homework. I flew to California and spent time with his life partner Don Bachardy at their home in Santa Monica Canyon. I reread Isherwood's novels. I read his diaries. When I was back in Manhattan, I walked the streets bundled in a cozy wool sweater, smoking cigarettes and speaking in a gentle transatlantic accent.

By the time I landed in the bracing prairie chill of Winnipeg, Manitoba, that November, I felt completely prepared for my scenes as one of several New York characters from Truman's literati clique.

Immediately upon arrival, I was informed that one of our group scenes had been cut. Disappointed that we were now down to four scenes, I carried on with my costume fittings and bonded with my fellow cast member David Rakoff (who played Gore Vidal).

My first scene was scheduled for late Saturday evening. The scene took place moments after Capote had finished a reading from his nonfiction masterpiece *In Cold Blood* to a packed theater in Manhattan. It took place in his dressing room, with a New York crowd laughing and celebrating.

The scene called for us to be interrupted by a tall man wearing a ridiculous hairpiece, who was to give Truman a flowery compliment. After his exit, I had a fun, comedic line about the hairpiece, which would end the scene.

I was called from my trailer, taken to the set, and seated in the center of a sofa, between Philip Seymour Hoffman and Bob Balaban—high company to be sure. I was nervous and excited, but prepared and ready to work.

As the crew finished tweaking the lights and positioning the extras, I noticed a tall, bald man standing in the doorway. The crew was taking longer than expected, so I went over and inquired if he was playing the man with the bad hairpiece.

Improvising and sweating it out with Philip Seymour Hoffman and Bob Balaban on the set of *Capote*.

Indeed he was. I asked the whereabouts of the hairpiece. He didn't know and said that makeup and hair didn't have one. How could this be? This was a UA/MGM/Sony Classics film! How could the hair and makeup department not have read the script and seen the funny line about the hairpiece?

Gingerly, I informed the director, Bennett Miller, about the missing hairpiece. He called for hair and makeup. They showed up empty-handed. Bennett then called for props and costumes, and a desperate hunt for some kind of comedy element was under way.

Here we were, on a cold Saturday evening in Winnipeg. Our chances of an open hair salon were zero. And not even the worst tie or bedazzled vest or outrageous boutonniere could be found, let alone turned into a comic moment.

Philip Seymour Hoffman was not happy, and an unhappy PSH was not a train you wanted to be in front of. I sat on the couch with Bob Balaban and watched Phil and Bennett discussing the matter with visible consternation. Was another of my scenes about to be cut? Reading my mind, Balaban said quietly, "Looks like we're going home early."

Over my dead body! I hadn't worked my ass off to have another scene cut. Also, Dan Futterman, the writer, was in Los Angeles and needed protecting. Someone had to save the scene! I summoned every ounce of courage and professionalism I had and walked toward Phil and Bennett. I was thinking, "Craig Archibald, if you're ever going to prove you belong here, it's now. Come on, think of something!"

Phil stopped his aggressive grumble and turned to glare at me. I shrugged and said in character as Christopher Isherwood, "Manhattan is not the place you want to be known as the village idiot."

Bennett said, "That's good!"

Phil said, "Keep going."

"Was that rather hairless gentleman your new paramour?"

They both smiled.

"Or perhaps your father?"

"Let's shoot," said Bennett.

Five minutes later, we were rolling film. We did nine or ten improvised takes of the scene. Phil and I struggled a bit at first, but after a few takes we found our way. After half an hour of intense work, we got a roar of laughter from Bennett and the gang watching the playback in the video village. We'd nailed the scene.

That night, soaking in the tub in my hotel room, I felt I'd achieved something important. I'd proven myself on a world-class film set. Negative moment turns positive. If I can do it, you can do it.

Sometimes It Really Hurts

Earlier in this book, I referenced the film *Kiss Me, Guido*. I've waited to tell this part of that story until now to illustrate one key point: this business can break your heart, but how you respond is what will define you.

In the winter of early 1995, I was originally cast in the lead role of "Warren" in the ultra-low-budget feature film *Kiss Me, Guido*. The writer/director, Tony Vitale, generously told me he'd been searching for me for a long time.

It was a mutual love affair! I felt like the role was written for me. The language, the humor, and the vulnerability were all a natural fit for me. We enjoyed our finding each other. Not just Tony and me but Warren and me as well.

All through that year of 1995, we did readings of the screenplay at different venues around Manhattan, trying to raise money to turn the dream of the film into a reality.

In one last desperate attempt to find backers, Tony flew to the Sundance Film Festival in January of 1996. There, he met Christine Vachon of Killer Films and Ira Deutchman of Fine Line Features. Both of them thought the script showed great promise and signed on. We were all very excited.

And then Paramount Pictures came on board. We weren't ultra-low-budget anymore.

Immediately, my unknown name became the center of a target. Tony valiantly demanded that I not be removed from my role, and Kerry Barden (the casting director) did his best to give me a shot, but in the end, the need for a "name" actor meant that I was demoted to a much smaller role.

I had lived for more than a year in Warren's shoes. I had committed months to working on his deepest motivations and secrets. This was the role I had been waiting for my whole life. I was Warren. I knew him inside and out. And yet, in the end, I wasn't.

The phone call from Kerry informing me that I didn't get the part broke my heart. My dream part went up in flames in less than twenty seconds. To his credit, Kerry was kind enough to call in person; casting directors usually leave the bad news to your agent or manager.

I was devastated. Shortly after the call, I blacked out in a passionate attack of rejection grief, only to wake up in my empty bathtub an hour later. How my queen mattress got off my bed and into the bathroom with me is still a mystery. My neighbor told me it sounded like I was giving birth.

But, in the end, I was cast in a Paramount movie. Everyone told me to be happy about it. It was a big step forward in my career. Ok. Sure. It was. But I still can't watch that movie.

What Is Success?

I've written this book to help you achieve success. But that raises an important question all actors need to ask: "What's my definition of success?"

Some people define success as if it's binary. You achieve a goal, or you don't. Win or lose. All or nothing. Such a mindset will guarantee you a short career in the arts. An auditioning actor might consider booking the role a win, failing to book it a loss. Your goals should certainly be focused and articulated, but judging the outcome in that binary way is unrealistic and limiting.

Success is defined by the Merriam Webster dictionary as "a desired outcome or result." The key word here is "desired." It suggests that you've thought about the outcome you want from your endeavors. It suggests it's not success unless you knew exactly what you desired and achieved it.

In reality, a life in the arts presents multiple types of success. If you're not specific about what you want, you could get all sorts of results. You could live in struggle and deprivation for years. You could luck out and get wonderful results quickly. Perhaps worst of all: you could luck out, become famous, then discover that you detest fame and celebrity and really didn't want it at all. I've seen it happen.

Let's not leave things to luck. Don't get me wrong: I think good luck is a blessing. The problem is that, by definition, you have no control over it. The Roman philosopher Seneca said, "Luck is what happens when preparation meets opportunity." It's an elegant way of saying that, to some extent at least, you can help shape your own luck. My clients who discipline themselves, prepare, and work hard to keep their acting tools sharp tend to be far more successful than those who are less adept at recognizing and seizing the opportunities that come their way.

And they do come, by the way. In my many years in this industry, I've rarely seen cases of truly committed actors who did not at one time or another get a quality opportunity. Their success, I've found, is generally proportional to their training and preparation, and the consequent quality of their work.

I want you to take control of your life. That means taking the time to define personal success and articulate exactly what you want from that success. Be specific. Make your choices unique and true to yourself. Success is meant to be fulfilling, gratifying, and exactly what you intended.

Make certain that your definition of success and your moral code are in alignment. Modern society has some peculiar, consumption-driven ideas about what success entails. Money's certainly nice—it buys you time and space—but no amount of money fills a creative or spiritual void.

I'll put it another way. It's important to stay grounded and realistic in your goals, rather than simply fantasizing. One of the assignments instructor Harold Baldridge gave me at the Neighborhood Playhouse was to read biographies of successful people in the arts.

It was good advice, because books such as *Montgomery Clift: A Biography*, *Lust for Life* (about the life of Vincent van Gogh), and *Hitchcock* by Francois Truffaut helped me understand the true nature of an artistic life—the ups and downs, the need for absolute commitment, the unexpected outcomes. The stories of other artists taught me to temper my expectations and acknowledge the many challenges artistic life entails. Read those books and many others.

A lot of young actors never realistically define what success looks like. They aspire to a vague dream of red carpets, Hollywood Hills infinity pools, and mirror-reflected Oscar speeches. They set themselves up for failure by insisting that anything short of that fantasy is a disappointment. I repeat, this is the recipe for brevity in an artistic career. The mindset you need for longevity in your career is one of realistic goals and detailed, personal ideas of what success means to you.

When you define success in highly personal terms, you do a couple of important things. First, you set yourself on a course. By defining a goal, you activate your attention toward the desired outcome. That in turn generates behavior from your motivational core, making it more likely that you'll achieve that goal.

Second, if you define success and then dig deep into the "why" behind it, you'll be rewarded with a new perspective that may surprise you. For example, if you said, "Success means I'll make a lot of money," I'd ask you to look deeply into why that would be wonderful. You might reply, "Well, it would free me from having to work a second job to support my craft." Or you might say, "It would let me take care of my family," or, "I'd be able to show my partner how much I love her by taking her on wonderful holidays."

Let me point out the three key words in those answers: "craft" and "family" and "love." If you dig into the reasons you define success in monetary terms, you may find that the "why" grows out of something deeper than material possessions: not just craft, family, and love, but things like art, integrity, compassion, authenticity, happiness, and health.

Defining success in this way gives you a wonderful gift! It helps you see that you may well be living a successful life already. If you're working on your craft with discipline and integrity, and taking care of your well-being, and tending your family and friendships with compassion and love, you're living your success. Right now.

When you shift your perspective to living in success, you'll experience a difference in life energy. You'll have a champion's energy. That energy can make a big difference in auditions and meetings. It can help you become even more successful.

Interrogate yourself. What will make your life more fulfilling? An expensive new car? A big house with no mortgage? Or immersion in craft, growing into your best self, living with integrity, helping people, telling stories, expressing your authentic heart, and creating a happy and healthy family (whatever that family is to you)? Understanding the deepest values that propel your life reveals the path of a long and healthy career.

Being driven is a good thing—but only to a point. If you squeeze your idea of success too tightly, you can strangle it. Give it room to morph and evolve and you'll be guided on your true journey.

I began my career with some definite ideas of what success would look like. I see now, looking back, how I limited myself. Happily, I've been guided by other values over the years that have enriched my definition of success.

As an actor and a writer, I had some lovely high-water marks and a few deep valleys. Some of these I've shared in this book. In my early forties, I hit a mid-life crisis. I was confronted with the reality that my career as an actor and writer wasn't likely to support me financially into my golden years. I needed to reorganize my life and figure out another way to live.

Back in 1995, I worked as a camera operator for the New York casting sessions of the film *Jerry Maguire*. A friend, actress Kathryn Erbe, informed me that she was coming in to read for the role of Dorothy Boyd (Renée Zellweger ultimately booked it). Katie was nervous and said, "Craig, you have to coach me on it."

Katie Erbe, my first coaching client and dear friend.

I had never coached anyone. The night before her audition, with considerable trepidation, I worked with her. We had a great time, and as we were winding up our session Katie kindly said, "You're a really good coach. You have a talent for it." I replied with a solid "Fuck you!" and we both laughed.

You see, to my immature ego, the idea of my being a coach meant that I was a complete failure. I was, after all, Craig Archibald! I was a Broadway-bound and future Oscar-winning world-class actor and soon-to-be legend!

But Katie was right. I do have a talent for it, a love of helping others grow, and a commitment to exploring and understanding the art form. Over time, coaching became not just a way for me to stop tending bar and waiting tables; it also gave me almost constant immersion in the discovery and definition of the craft, discipline, and business of acting.

Gradually, coaching became the answer to my mid-life crisis. When I moved from Manhattan to Malibu in 2007, I also made the professional adjustment to full-time acting coach. It took lots of personal work to temper the ego I'd attached to my career as an actor and writer, and to accept coaching as a considered option rather than a future arrived at by default.

As it turned out, coaching led me on an immensely rewarding spiritual journey. In time I came into flow, into the Zen zone. Weeks and months of work go by these days as I work with actors at the Archibald Studio, and all I feel is the beautiful now—the joy of truthfully living in the discovery of every creative moment.

I found that I haven't limited myself by becoming an acting coach— quite the opposite. Paradoxically, coaching, which I feared would narrow my life, has opened it up. I am connected to more writers, directors, producers, agents, managers, casting directors, and actors than ever before. Each day is new and exciting. Unexpected opportunities come my way.

I now find myself happily coaching, mentoring, spending time with family and friends, producing, writing, and working on my beloved craft of acting every day. That's how I've come to define success for myself. How do you define success?

Don't be the idea of what you think you should be.

Be the imperfect good thing that you are.

And do not be afraid to be your best.

Acknowledgments

I have many people to thank in writing this book, the majority of whom are my clients. Thank you for inspiring me through the years. You have truly taught me as much as I've taught you. To those of you who have become friends as well as clients (you know who you are), please take this book as a sincere celebration of the artistic life we share.

My colleague and dear friend Dan Futterman was one of the first on this train, encouraging me to write what I was coaching. Our buddy Ali Selim enthusiastically backed him up. When Kim Peacock heard about it, she became a passionate champion, and finally Michael Albanese jumped on the support express, and there's been no looking back. You made this happen, my friends. Thank you.

Key people offered their input, read early drafts, and improved them. These include Lathrop Walker, my brother Kim Archibald (thanks for your honesty, brother!), and Gary Ross, who taught me many things, in his early edit help. Erik Odom takes a special spot in this lineup as a truly adept line editor, sounding board, sage soul, and buddy. He also just edited that line.

I wish to thank Marty Beller for introducing me, many years ago, to his lovely wife and now my literary agent Jill Grinberg. What fun that we would one day team up to enjoy this journey together. My gratitude to you, Jill, is profound. Plus, we laugh. Thank you also to Jill's amazing team in Brooklyn, in particular Sophia Seidner and Denise Page.

Thank you also to Jill for landing me with the team at Applause Theatre and Cinema books. John Cerullo is a champion of common sense, artistic sensitivity, and knowhow. His extraordinary team of Carol Flannery, Chris Chappell, Barbara Claire, Laurel Myers, Naomi Minkoff, Jo-Ann Parks, and

Jessica Kastner certainly helped this first-time author through the maze of book publishing with kindness, attention to detail, and professionalism.

Career support from these entertainment industry professionals was significant and meaningful: Gloria Bonelli, Peggy Hadley, John Lyons, and Marc Isaacman. A special shout-out of gratitude to my two legal eagles, Anne Friedman and June Dietrich.

Thank you to Constance Wu for trusting me with your work, your friendship, and gracing me with your very kind words.

My staff at the Archibald Studio is vital to my survival. Thank you for being patient with me, Berda Gilmore, Christina Piazza, Kathy Dorn, and Ricky Oakley. A special nod of thanks to Keong Sim, Megan Heyn, Lane Aikin, Anthony Rey Perez, Ashley Brown, Lisa Cordelione, and Josh Heisler, the best backup team a guy could dream of.

I got really lucky in my life twice. Once was to meet MaryCay Durrant and the second was to meet Les McGehee. You held my hand and led me through the rapids of becoming an entrepreneur. Your grace, kindness, and wisdom are the very foundation of my business. My gratitude is limitless.

Our fellow artists make our lives sane, safe, and inspired. My deepest gratitude to my life-long artistic warrior buddies Kevin Stapleton, Maggie Moore, Katie Erbe, Brian Foyster, Lucy Avery Brooke, Betsy Currie, Anya Epstein, Ann Olsson, Matt Mayer, Scoop Wasserstein, David Driver, Jason Tougaw, Peter Brown, Vesti Hanson, Cam McConnell, Jeff Rogstad, Angus Ferguson, Mark Melymick, Amy Stiller, Elizabeth Ziff, Susie Mosher, Lothaire Bluteau, Gale Harold, Jeff Lipsky, and Gary Lennon. Now that's an all-star lineup!

Amy Shock and Susie Crippen deserve special mention not only for our friendships but also for the sharing of their respective homes for me to spend weekends and holidays squirreled away throwing items at my computer.

Several families have openly embraced me and included me in their lives. As an immigrant living in a new country, your gracious and generous hospitality has meant more to me than you may ever know. Thank you to Carol and Bill McNulty, the Stapletons, the Crippens, the Futtermans, and the Epsteins. In Canada, the Johnson, Larocque, Bond, Zoerb, and Moore clans have always been a deep source of comfort and support.

I have had the great fortune to have many wonderful teachers and mentors. They include Robert Hinitt, Kathy Bond, Jim Guedo, Ronald (Bingo) Mavor, Henry Woolf, Ian McKellen, Sanford Meisner, Harold Baldridge, Robert Xavier Modica, and Suzanne Shepherd. If there's a spiritual vibrancy to gratitude, it sings here.

My inner circle of Maureen Finkle, Lisa Warner, Barbie and Trevor Cross, Patrick Collins, Sarah James, Derek Norman, Peter Crippen, Susan and Larry DellaRatta, Todd Bellucci, Ingrid Mavor, Tim Gleason, Emily Houpt, Victor Zelek, Andy and Jack Kiernan, Jim Likens, Wynn Everett, Keene McRae, Cedric Sanders, Alyssa Sutherland, Tyson Turrou, Austin Hebert, Victor Sanchez, and Amy Gumenick are the support center all artistic endeavors require but rarely find.

One special salute to Megan Johnson who has been a wonderful pal and pandemic pod partner! Charmed, I'm sure.

I'm the luckiest Uncle Craig in the world. My pack of nieces and nephews (blood related and not) are not only dear friends; they also make me a better man every day.

And finally, to my dear siblings, Kim, Mary, Colleen, Robin, and Diane (and their beloved families), the love in my heart for you is as big as the sky above the farm in Steep Creek . . . endless.

Index

CPSIA information can be obtained
at www.ICGtesting.com
Printed in the USA
BVHW091354110222
628344BV00004B/11